GOOD

FINDING HEALTHY **BALANCE**

IN

IN A CULTURE OF **EXTREMES**

TENSION

Copyright © 2024 by Jeremy Yancey

Published by Arrows and Stones

All rights reserved. No portion of this book may be reproduced, stored in a retrieval system, or transmitted in any form or by any means—electronic, mechanical, photocopy, recording, scanning, or other—except for brief quotations in critical reviews or articles, without prior written permission of the author.

Unless otherwise marked, all Scripture quotations are taken from the Holy Bible, New International Version®. Copyright © 1973, 1978, 1984, 2011 by Biblica, Inc.™ Used by permission of Zondervan. All rights reserved worldwide. www.zondervan.com. The "NIV" and "New International Version" are trademarks registered in the United States Patent and Trademark Office by Biblica, Inc.™ | Scripture quotations marked BSB are from The Holy Bible, Berean Study Bible, BSB, Copyright ©2016, 2020 by Bible Hub Used by Permission. All Rights Reserved Worldwide. | Scripture quotations marked CSB have been taken from the Christian Standard Bible®, Copyright © 2017 by Holman Bible Publishers. Used by permission. Christian Standard Bible® and CSB® are federally registered trademarks of Holman Bible Publishers. | Scripture quotations marked GNT are from the Good News Translation in Today's English Version- Second Edition Copyright © 1992 by American Bible Society. Used by Permission. | All Scripture marked with the designation GW is taken from GOD'S WORD®. © 1995, 2003, 2013, 2014, 2019, 2020 by God's Word to the Nations Mission Society. Used by permission. | Scripture quotations marked KJV are taken from the King James Version of the Bible. Public domain. | | Scripture quotations marked MSG are taken from THE MESSAGE, copyright © 1993, 1994, 1995, 1996, 2000, 2001, 2002 by Eugene H. Peterson. Used by permission of NavPress. All rights reserved. Represented by Tyndale House Publishers, Inc. | Scripture quotations marked NASB are taken from the (NASB®) New American Standard Bible®, Copyright © 1960, 1971, 1977, 1995, 2020 by The Lockman Foundation. Used by permission. All rights reserved. www.lockman.org | | Scripture quotations marked NKJV are taken from the New King James Version®. Copyright © 1982 by Thomas Nelson. Used by permission. All rights reserved. | Scripture quotations marked NLT are taken from the Holy Bible, New Living Translation, copyright © 1996, 2004, 2015 by Tyndale House Foundation. Used by permission of Tyndale House Publishers, Inc., Carol Stream, Illinois 60188. All rights reserved. | Scripture quotations marked ESV are taken from The Holy Bible, English Standard Version. ESV® Text Edition: 2016. Copyright © 2001 by Crossway Bibles, a publishing ministry of Good News Publishers. Used by permission. | Scripture quotations marked NRSV are taken from New Revised Standard Version, Updated Edition. Copyright © 2021 National Council of Churches of Christ in the United States of America. Used by permission. All rights reserved worldwide.

For foreign and subsidiary rights, contact the author.

Cover design by Sara Young
Cover photo by Kellie Gann

ISBN: 978-1-960678-38-6   1 2 3 4 5 6 7 8 9 10

Printed in the United States of America

GOOD

FINDING HEALTHY **BALANCE**

IN

IN A CULTURE OF **EXTREMES**

TENSION

JEREMY YANCEY

ARROWS & STONES

CONTENTS

Foreword vii

CHAPTER 1. **A Tension Deficit** 11

CHAPTER 2. **Flexible Focus** 31

CHAPTER 3. **Real Hope** 51

CHAPTER 4. **Humbly Confident** 65

CHAPTER 5. **Candid And Kind** 83

CHAPTER 6. **Running And Resting** 99

CHAPTER 7. **Listening and Speaking** 119

CHAPTER 8. **In-Tension-al Living** 135

CHAPTER 9. **A Prayer That's Taut** 155

FOREWORD

We live in a world that can't stand tension. When things were tough at the Alamo, Colonel Travis drew a line in the sand with his sword and asked people to choose: with us or not. In the same way, many Christians are drawing lines in the sand on every conceivable issue, and they conclude that those who stay on their side are always right, and those who are on the other side are always wrong—and not just wrong: evil. The result is that many of us who claim to know the love of Christ see those "on the other side" as beyond redemption—and they know it.

Walking in tension is one of the hardest but most necessary tasks for believers today, and my friend Jeremy has shared his experience and insights about it in this book. This may not be the easiest book to read because he challenges our unwillingness to "see the other side."

If you want to grow to new levels of spiritual depth with God, you'll need to embrace tension because it's found throughout the

Bible. For instance, we're described as both sinners and saints. God is ultimately sovereign, but He has given us responsibility for our choices. We are to "seek the peace of the city" and "stand against injustice." And our doubts are often the path to greater faith. Jesus was called "a friend of sinners" (Matthew 11:19), and He calls us to follow Him in being a friend of sinners too. Very practically, this means that if I'm at a ball game, the gym, a coffee shop, or anywhere else, and I get into a conversation with someone who holds a different view than mine, I'm *not* mandated to draw the line like Colonel Travis. I am mandated to navigate the tension. Instead of shutting down or heating up, I can do the following:

› Take a deep breath, so I have a second to think instead of just reacting.
› Invite them with, "Tell me how you see it." (I saw a cartoon of two people sitting on opposite sides of a table looking at a number. One of them says, "I see a 6." The other insists, "No, it's a 9!" One of them should have said, "Let me come to your side of the table, so I can see what you see.") Far too often, we live in "echo chambers," listening only to people say what we already believe. That's called confirmation bias, and it prevents us from understanding people who have different views.
› Ask questions—not accusatory questions, not questions meant to make the person look foolish, and not questions that have no answers. Ask . . . and listen. I know I'm really listening if I ask follow-up questions instead of waiting for a breath, so I can jump in with my opinion. Later in the book, Jeremy unpacks the tension between how to listen and when to speak.

› And after you've listened well, ask, "Would you mind if I explain my point of view?" If you've been gracious enough to listen, the person will almost always return the favor. Again, share your opinion without demanding agreement—embrace the tension. I'm not suggesting that you compromise your values and principles, only that you take the time to understand the other person. You'll have a far better chance of changing other people's opinions if they feel understood instead of attacked. Here's a benchmark: Listen and ask questions well enough so that you can explain the other person's point of view so well that she says, "Yes, that's exactly what I believe!" Remember, you don't have to agree with someone to learn from them, be kind to them, treat them with respect, and be a genuine friend.

I've found that if we take that first step, God often works to bring understanding, resolution, repentance, and reconciliation. But we need to find the courage to take that first step.

We live in a world full of tension. Learning to navigate it well requires a powerful blend of humility and courage . . . candor and kindness . . . laser focus and healthy flexibility. That's what Jeremy's book is all about. I have the utmost respect for him. He is a compassionate, intentional leader who communicates powerful convictions with great love.

—Scott Wilson
Global Pastor, The Oaks
Red Oak, Texas

CHAPTER 1

A TENSION DEFICIT

The last thing I expected to hear in that moment were *those six words* blurted from my overtly observant, usually well-behaved, but incredibly naïve four-year-old son.

It was a warm and muggy spring afternoon in East Texas. My son Graham and I were on our way to one of his many T-ball games. He was decked out in his uniform, buckled up in his car seat, beautifully serenading me to another round of the smash hit song "What Does the Fox Say?" (The only reason I call it a smash hit is because you want to smash or hit something after you've heard it more than thrice.)

As we pulled up to one of the stoplights en route to the ball field, both of our attentions abruptly moved away from what the fox was saying to a young woman, crossing the very busy street at the light. She was nicely dressed in business attire but walking barefoot through the intersection, holding her heels in one hand while handling a stack of textbooks with the other. In the direction she was walking, the sidewalk was ending, and the only place left to go was the shoulder of the busy highway. I don't make a habit of inviting young college girls off the shoulder of the highway and into my vehicle. But I felt like my "stranger danger" vibe was low enough with my son in the backseat that I could at least see if she needed any help.

I pulled onto the shoulder next to her and said, "Hey there! I don't want to freak you out . . . just want to see if you're all right?"

"I'm okay," she said. "My mom wasn't able to come pick me up from my speech class, so I'm just walking home."

I asked her how far home was, and she said, "Only about six miles!" After telling her I had my son in the back, I was a pastor of a local church, and that I hadn't murdered anyone lately, I offered her a ride home, and she gladly accepted.

As she shut the front passenger door, my son immediately became very quiet. I could see him in the rearview, inquisitively examining our new passenger and listening intently as I attempted a little small talk with our new friend. What was she studying? How long did she have left before graduating the local community college? Which house was hers down this street? A distance of one hundred yards from her driveway was apparently the cue for my son to interject the massive observation he had made and had been undoubtedly wrestling with in his mind for the past 5.9 miles.

Without any warning, from the confines of his car seat, Graham made the following announcement:

"You know? Some ladies have beards!"

It wasn't that my son's words were inappropriate, per se. They were just terribly inconvenient because our new friend (who was only twenty-five seconds away from being dropped off) just so happened to be one of those ladies that, you know, had some unruly facial hair. I'm not saying she would've been hired by the carnival, but it was an immediately noticeable trait in her appearance. Apparently, the Texas sun was beaming through the front windshield like a prison searchlight, highlighting this young woman's five o'clock shadow in such a way that my son simply assumed this was nothing less than a divine illumination his world needed to know immediately!

Although she seemed unfazed, I was not. And as Graham seemed like he was gearing up to say more, I awkwardly interrupted him and began to fill the car with loud nonsensical gibberish that sounded something like "a riiiing ding ding a ding a aring a ding!" The only thing my brain could come up with in that moment were the lyrics to "What Does the Fox Say?"

You could cut the tension with a knife—or a Gillette razor.

TOUGH CALLS

Have you ever been there? Right in the middle of a tense situation? I'm talking about *thick* tension. Attending your daughter's piano recital, and she pauses midpiece because she's forgotten the next stanza. You want to jump in and help her, but you can't.

Or you're on a double date that becomes a scene from a recent Desperate Housewives of Chattanooga when the other couple decides to get into that argument that just won't stop. (Or maybe you were that couple and just didn't know it.)

Or the unavoidable family reunion where Uncle Jack keeps trying to show you the scar from his recent colon surgery.

Maybe it's even deeper. Maybe you've had to navigate the holiday knowing that you and a relative are very much at odds with each other. You don't want to say too much. You don't want to say too little. So you tiptoe and sidestep while others sense the tension too.

Whether you were a participant or a bystander, you have surely felt the discomfort of situations like this. How can you respond? What should you say? Is there any way out? What would the fox say?

And what about the kind of tension that comes not from a bad situation but from a tough decision between two good options?

Say yes to the promotion, and you'll have to uproot your family for a move across the country. Say no, and get stuck in the company's grid—missing out on opportunities that might benefit your family over the long term.

There's no clear right or wrong here, but the tension is still strong. Both responses seem to have good and bad consequences attached. You feel torn. How should you respond?

If you're a Christ-follower, trying to figure out God's will, there are moments when you open the Scripture and read, "This is the way . . . walk and talk and live like this." But in other moments, there are no clear answers, no succinct directions. You have to choose, and that decision-making can bring, you know, tension.

Tension is tough. We don't like it. We try to avoid it. Like the strain in a relationship, a delicate situation at work, or Uncle Jack at the reunion. No one automatically puts tension in the win column. But would you believe me if I told you: Tension can be a good thing?

Would you believe me if I told you: Tension can be a good thing?

Consider the beautiful sound generated by an expert guitarist. The strings are stretched taut. Each one has its level of tension. The guitarist's fingers work their way across the strings, adding tension here and there, making the instrument sing.

Now imagine that guitarist is Eric Clapton, playing his song "Tears in Heaven." It's a hauntingly beautiful sound, all the more heartrending when we realize he composed it in response to the death of his four-year-old child. Not only are Clapton's fingers working with the tension of the instrument to produce sound, but as a songwriter, he has created an exquisite ballad based on his personal tension.

In a physical way, we rely on various tensions throughout our lives. We can think of the human body as a complex system of pulleys, belts, and gears. Without healthy tension, your body would collapse to the floor. Tension keeps it moving in the right way.

Emotional, mental, and spiritual tensions can also serve to make us stronger. These tensions are not pleasant. We often try to avoid them. But we ultimately recognize the growth that results.

When it comes to living a life for Christ, there is such a thing as healthy tension.

In this book, I want to help you turn the dial, drill down, ratchet up, and tune in to a different understanding of tension. Instead of viewing tension through a negative lens, I want us to embrace tension as a positive force, creating a counterbalance that brings fullness to our lives.

And that's exactly what Christ wants for us. "I have come that they may have life, and have it to the full," He said (John 10:10).

COUNTERBALANCE IN THE BIBLE

Once we understand the principle of healthy tension, we start seeing it throughout Scripture.

In Matthew 10:16 (NKJV), Jesus sent His disciples out in ministry, challenging them to "be wise as serpents and harmless as doves." Consider the tension involved in that pairing. A serpent strikes quickly. It's fierce, agile. A dove is calm, peaceful, pure. The Bible says we're supposed to be some of both. A "life to the fullest" (see John 10:10) balances between healthy tensions.

We see Jesus described as both a lamb and a lion (see John 1:28 and Revelation 5:5) and approachable yet unbelievably powerful. The king—and an animal to be sacrificed.

In James 1:19, we're told that "everyone should be quick to listen, slow to speak and slow to become angry." Quick and slow. Listen actively. Energetically understand. But frame your responses carefully. Don't fly off the handle.

I'm intrigued by two back-to-back proverbs that seem to say opposite things:

> *"Do not answer a fool according to his folly, or you yourself will be just like him. Answer a fool according to his folly, or he will be wise in his own eyes."* —Proverbs 26:4-5

So, what do we learn here? Should we answer a fool or not?

This isn't a contradiction—it's wisdom in action. Be careful about jumping into foolish conversations, but you might want to express genuine concern for a person who's talking foolishly.

We find balancing acts like this in most books of the Bible. We are cautioned against extremes that are sinful or dangerous, but we're invited to live, with God's guidance, in the tension between two acceptable states.

How does this work? Are we constantly bouncing back and forth, like those who are "double-minded and unstable in all they do" (James 1:8)?

No, I think there's a big difference between vacillating and oscillating.

> *There's a big difference between vacillating and oscillating.*

When I vacillate, I'm like a bullet ricocheting, engaging in disorganized and dangerous movement without any purpose. Like my eighth-grade self, doing the Macarena to impress Sadie Jackson at the middle school prom. Not a pretty picture.

But when I oscillate, I move with purpose between two points. Like the wide swath covered by the spotlight of a light tower. Back and forth it goes, covering a range of territory. It's not fixed on one spot but illuminates a wide area. When we show that same range in our attitudes and actions, we display maturity.

I think of the apostle Paul saying, "I have become all things to all people so that by all possible means I might save some" (1 Corinthians 9:22). He wasn't masquerading as someone he was not. He was oscillating. And we see this as we track his ministry in the book of Acts. He could speak powerfully as a rabbi in a synagogue or quietly as a philosopher in Athens. He adopted different personal styles in his strategic efforts to get the gospel across.

Consider the subtle but succinct movement of a balancing pole in the hands of an acrobat traversing a tightrope. It is absolutely essential for that person to stay centered on that wire. So isn't it odd to use a pole that stretches broadly to either side? The acrobat understands that balance requires a healthy tension between one side and the other and maintaining that tension.

This book is about walking that tightrope.

EVERYDAY LIFE

If tension is truly a normal part of life, it will be an ingredient in the Christ-centered life. Let's pause here a moment and see what Paul says in Romans 12. (I love the vivid imagery *The Message* paraphrase finds in the words of the original languages.)

> *So here's what I want you to do, God helping you: Take your everyday, ordinary life—your sleeping, eating, going-to-work, and walking-around life—and place it before God as an offering.* —Romans 12:1

Slow down a moment. Take a snapshot of your life; then pinch your fingers on the picture and zoom in a little bit. What kind of life do these verses describe? Is this some extreme of religious devotion? No! It's "ordinary, everyday life" that's offered up to God. The Greek text uses a normal word for our physical bodies

A TENSION DEFICIT

(somata) and a normal word for living (zosan) to encompass all these ordinary activities—sleeping, eating, etc. This is the life we give back to God—lived within our normal tensions but letting God establish our healthy balance. If we live and move and have our being in Him, He will fill our lives.

But wait; there's more. Reading on in Romans 12, we find:
Embracing what God does for you is the best thing you can do for him. Don't become so well-adjusted to your culture that you fit into it without even thinking. Instead, fix your attention on God. You'll be changed from the inside out. Readily recognize what he wants from you, and quickly respond to it. Unlike the culture around you, always dragging you down to its level of immaturity, God brings the best out of you, develops well-formed maturity in you. —Romans 12:2 (MSG)

That's what I want for my kids and my wife and for me. I want us to learn the code for counterbalance. I want us to practice the rhythm of oscillation within several everyday practical and emotional tensions rather than just fitting into the wildly vacillating extremes of culture that derail us from pivotal friendships, damage our communities, and deprive us of our potential influence.

Is it challenging? Uh, heck yes. And we will explore how to navigate those challenges in each chapter. But this ongoing, ever-changing, consistently inconsistent pull between two extremes has the capacity to produce a full and vibrant life in Christ that changes how we look at the world—and can also, in fact, change the world.

GOING TO EXTREMES

"Extremes" are the enemy of healthy tension. These days, you don't have to search long on FaceTube or Tik-chat to find people talking about extreme things in extreme ways.

> *"Extremes" are the enemy of healthy tension.*

Just this morning, I read a post on a community Facebook page from someone who was absolutely terrified. She had awakened in the middle of the night to find an elderly woman standing at the foot of her bed, yelling, "Where's Annie?" Then this mystery woman ran out the back door.

Talk about a tense situation—not to mention absurd and troubling! But what I found even more absurd and troubling—and all too common—was the first comment on her post from a random stranger: "Why are you sleeping with your doors unlocked?" Then someone else chimed in to yell at this woman at the top of their thumbs on how stupid she was not to call the police (though the original post clearly stated that she had done so). The third comment hit a creepy new low with a random guy offering to keep her "company" that night if she got scared.

Three ridiculous comments, but are they really that shocking? Sadly, no. I think I helped the situation by writing, "I hope Annie's okay."

That seems to be the culture we're living in, doesn't it? We are quick to jump to extreme conclusions, extreme opinions, extreme solutions, and extreme emotions.

It's almost like we're addicted to it. We have a tension deficit. We lack healthy tension.

When Jesus offered us life "to the full" in John 10:10, He wasn't pushing us to these extremes of judgment, anger, shaming, or verbal abuse. He called us to love God with all we've got and to love our neighbors as ourselves. Also, to love our enemies. These might be considered extreme challenges in their own way, but they're grounded in a vital relationship with God—a God who created us to exist within healthy tensions. "In him we live and move and have our being," Acts 17:28 (ESV) says.

God wants you to have an incredibly full life, like a bouquet of flowers whose vibrant colors can be enjoyed from all sides. Extreme thinking dismisses any other angle. We don't hear the healthy tension from the taut strings of a well-tuned guitar—only the raucous shouts insulting those who disagree.

IRON MAN

I have not mastered healthy tensions. Far from it. All too often, I chase after extremes, and that hurts my work, my relationships, even my health. I tend to be an all-or-nothing person. I can binge-watch TV better than anybody. But I've also set physical goals for myself, and I go all out.

Have you heard of the Iron Man competition? It's a grueling endeavor that includes a 2.4-mile swim, a 112-mile bike ride, and a full marathon (26.2 miles). Less than 1 percent of 1 percent of athletes have ever completed an Iron Man. In past years, I've ramped up, doing three half Iron Man competitions. Last year, I decided to go for the full-length Iron Man. I hired a coach. I started getting up religiously before 4 a.m. to swim, bike, and run. I'd be in the pool at the local athletic club before the sun rose and finish up just as the "Swimming with the Oldies" ladies' class started pushing me out of their space. I'd finish up Sunday services, take a nap, then jump on the indoor bike trainer for seven hours as my wife had friends over to play dominoes and eat pizza in the other room. I'm not bitter. Okay, I'm bitter-ish. But I'm getting offtrack.

I went to an unhealthy extreme.

Pushing myself in physical training, plus the dynamic challenges and opportunities of church life, family responsibilities, ball games, and college prep for our oldest—I simply created an unsustainable burden. Besides the scheduling issues and the emotional challenges, I pushed too hard physically. My body began to experience injuries, making it impossible to run, derailing my training, and scrapping my goals.

I've learned the hard way that I shouldn't take everything to the extreme. I had put an enormous amount of importance on that singular goal, never imagining any other outcome. Even now, as I write this, I'm feeling the disappointment.

The apostle Paul wrote to his protégé, Timothy, that "physical training is of some value, but godliness has value for all things, holding promise for both the present life and the life to come" (1 Timothy 4:8). Can you hear the balanced perspective Paul was sharing with Tim? Me too. I should have learned it earlier. Yes, there is "some value" in pushing my body, but there's eternal value in striking a godly balance in my life, being there for my family, and advancing the growth of my church.

> Yes, there is "some value" in pushing my body, but there's eternal value in striking a godly balance in my life, being there for my family, and advancing the growth of the church.

Let's be clear. I'm not saying—and neither was Paul saying—that physical training is bad. But we need to keep it in balance, and certainly not be consumed by it.

BALANCED LIKE BRIDEZILLA

Weddings can be lovely events, with beautiful gowns and tuxes donned, majestic music played, meaningful words proclaimed, and everyone on his or her best-ish behavior. But then there's the character we've come to know as Bridezilla. She breathes fire, destroying people in her path, because she craves the perfect wedding.

There is nothing balanced about a Bridezilla. She has dreamed of this event all her life, and she's not going to let anyone keep her from having it. Every detail—flowers, cake, venue—must rise to her impeccable and, more than likely, impossible standards.

But what's really happening here? Her demanding behavior is threatening relationships with her family and closest friends—including the man she hopes to spend her life married to. (More than one groom has had second thoughts, not because of cold feet, but because wedding planning has revealed a side of the bride he hadn't seen before.) In order to make one day, one event, a few hours on a Saturday afternoon special, a usually balanced bride has the capacity to breathe fire onto her whole world—possibly doing damage to other moments, events, and days far into the future.

Perhaps you've attended a wedding on the opposite extreme, one that was poorly planned, where details were neglected. The ceremony started late. The preacher went too long (okay, don't judge). The caterer arrived late. The bride consumed a little too much liquid courage coupled with a Xanax and could barely make it down the aisle. (True story—I was the officiant. It was a beautiful mess-terpiece.)

So we could set up a grid. At one extreme is Bridezilla whose perfectionism creates terror. At the other extreme is Apathy whose utter lack of planning creates a bad experience for everyone. But there are options in the middle—not a single midpoint, but two—what we might call Careful Planner and Relaxed Planner.

Bridezilla–Careful Planner–Relaxed Planner–Apathetic

Careful Planner pays attention to details, communicating her desire for a great wedding to everyone involved. But no fire-breathing. Relaxed Planner understands that the event won't be perfect but still wants to create a good experience for her guests and for posterity.

A healthy tension exists between those two central poles. Both are healthy positions, but they often improve by moving toward the other pole and away from the extreme. The groom tells his Careful Planner bride-to-be, "Relax! It'll be fine." The mother of the Relaxed Planner bride says, "Maybe we should serve appetizers while people wait for the photos to be taken."

FINDING HEALTHY TENSION IN THE MIDDLE

In this book, I point to six different sets of characteristics. In each case, there are two central qualities that are quite different from each other, but both are good. Many people in my life lean one way or the other, including me. (You might want to take a few minutes now to consider your own leanings.) We'll be examining each of these pairs and the healthy tension that can exist between them.

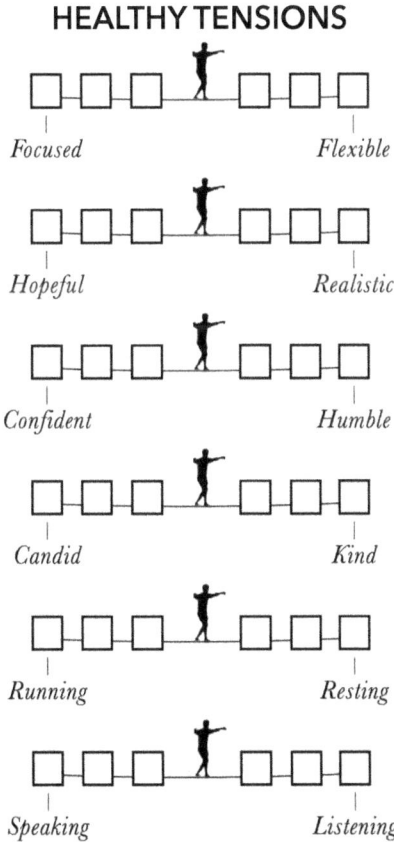

We also see the Bridezilla pattern I described earlier. Any of these qualities could be taken to an unhealthy extreme.

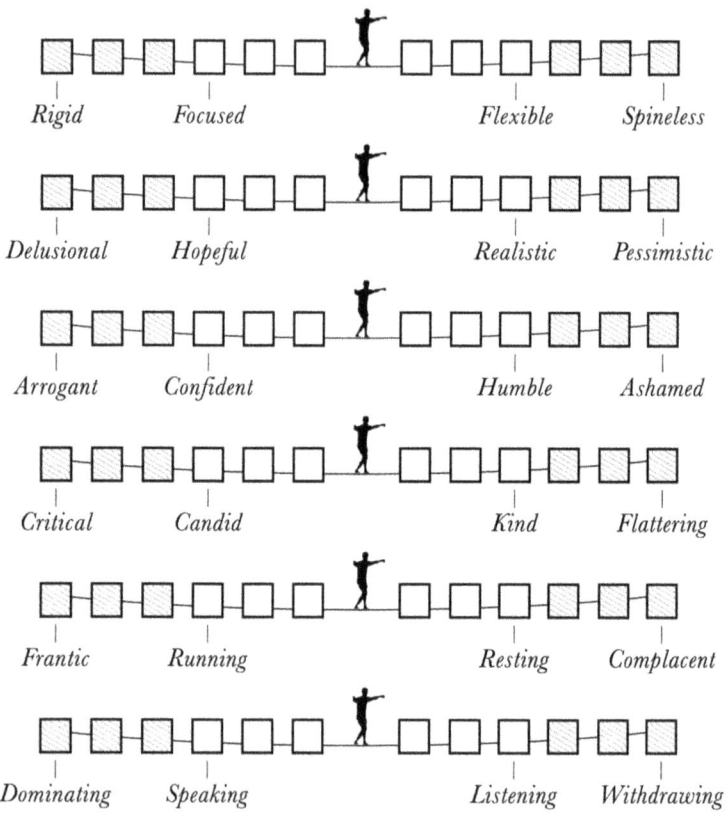

HEALTHY TENSIONS WITH UNHEALTHY EXTREMES

People do a lot of damage to themselves and others when they adopt extreme positions in these areas. Perhaps the worst thing is that they deny themselves that healthy tension with the opposite characteristic. Bridezilla doesn't want to hear from Relaxed Planner. Relaxation has no part in her plans. Instead of having a helpful conversation about careful and relaxed planning, the extremists assume they have nothing to learn from anybody. They breathe fire on anyone who thinks differently.

> *Don't read what I'm not saying.*
> *I'm not dictating one position*
> *as the absolute place to be.*

Don't read what I'm not saying. I'm not dictating one position as the absolute place to be. You may be careful or relaxed, but live within that tension. You may naturally be "Focused," or you might like to do life in a more "Flexible" way. What would it look like to stay open to options from the opposite side? What if you could intentionally invite people into your life who occupy that other spot and listen to them? You might not need to change your focused ways, but there might be times when a flexible choice will work better.

Maybe you're the "Realistic" voice in every staff meeting, explaining why some new plan probably won't work. Great. That's an important role. That team will also benefit from the thoughts of the "Hopeful" person across the table. The very God of the cosmos shows us the way things really are, but He also invites us to put our hope in His miraculous work. Wisdom resides in a well-balanced tension between these viewpoints.

So it is with other aspects of our personalities. You may have formed a deep friendship or two (or even a marriage) with someone who differs from you in some key area. Maybe they're very patient while you're driven to get things done. Maybe you don't want to hurt anyone's feelings, but they bluntly tell people what they "need to know."

Perhaps you've argued over these differences, but over time, you've learned to embrace a healthy tension. You can be a good influence on each other, guarding against the extremes on either side. The goal is not to become identical but to use your differences to enrich one another's life.

THE CENTER OF THE STORM

If you live for Christ long enough, there will be moments when you feel you are in the palm of God's hand. Your ear is to the chest of God, and you can hear your Creator's heartbeat. Everything is under control.

Then there are other moments of chaos when you can't quite see your next step. Life is volatile, constantly in motion. You feel like you're on a boat . . . in a storm . . . on the Sea of Galilee . . . while Jesus is asleep in the stern. Remember that story? The disciples were freaking out. They woke Jesus up, yelling, "Don't you care?" (Mark 4:38).

As you may recall, Jesus spoke peace to the storm. He does the same in our stormy situations. Life may drive us to extremes, but Jesus pulls us back to the center, to our center, to our trust in Him. That trust requires a tension of leaning on Him and leaning not on our own understanding.

HEALTHY TENSION: Jesus wants to help you find it and live in it. On our own, we're prone to extreme reactions to the storms and chaos of life. Jesus is always inviting us back to a centered, surrendered trust in Him. He is our horizon point. The lighthouse. The fulcrum that will recalibrate our tension deficit.

HEALTHY TENSION: Jesus wants to help you find it and live in it.

CHAPTER 2

FLEXIBLE FOCUS

Peter was doing the impossible. Walking on water.

In Matthew 14:22-32, Jesus had sent His disciples by boat across the Sea of Galilee while He went off alone to pray. The boat had sailed "a considerable distance" (verse 24) from shore when a storm blew up. The sea was churning. And the disciples saw a mysterious figure walking toward them—on top of the waves. Some thought it was a ghost, perhaps warning them of a dangerous sea.

As the waves continued to toss their boat, the frightened disciples heard a voice calling to them. It was the voice of Jesus, saying what He often said: "Don't be afraid" (verse 27). Peter, already gaining a reputation for acting before thinking, called back, "Lord, if it's you, tell me to come to you on the water" (verse 28).

The Master invited His impetuous student to join Him. As Matthew describes it, "Then Peter got down out of the boat, walked on the water and came toward Jesus" (verse 29).

After reading the Gospels numerous times, we get used to the miracles of Jesus. He was always wowing the public, dazzling His disciples. Walking on water is just one more item on a stellar résumé. But Peter! He must have been pumped! What would this feel like, step-by-step, being borne up by the water? As a fisherman, he knew how water worked. It swallowed people up. Fall out of a boat, and you sink. But he wasn't sinking. He was stepping on the waves like a, well, like a god. And with every step, he was getting closer and closer to Jesus.

Until he wasn't.

Something changed for Peter (verse 30): "But when he saw the wind, he was afraid and, beginning to sink, cried out, 'Lord, save me!'"

Simply stated, Peter lost his focus.

Simply stated, Peter lost his focus. As long as his attention was riveted on Jesus, he was fine, but when the wind distracted him, he sank. Jesus reached out a hand and saved him, then chided him for his lack of faith.

It was one of many learning opportunities for Peter, and before we slam him for doubting, remember that there were eleven other guys who never left the boat. Maybe an important part of the life lesson for Peter was this: "Imagine how cool it could be if you kept your focus on Me all the time."

COMING INTO FOCUS

It's estimated that three-quarters of American adults wear glasses or contact lenses. If you're one of them, you know the joy of having an eye doctor try out various lenses: "Is this better, or *this*? How about *this*?"

"That's blurry," you might say. "It's not in focus." And the doctor flicks a lever to make things clearer.

We might also consider the importance of mental focus. Millions of children and adults worldwide have been diagnosed with attention deficits, and many more are undiagnosed but show symptoms. Even if you're not in this group, you've probably experienced unfocused thinking after a sleepless night or a boring lecture. You might even be reading this sentence right now, and you realize that you can't really remember the last four sentences you just read because you started wondering when the last time was you got your own eyes checked and if your prescription has expired. And speaking of expiring, I need to return those six items to Amazon before the thirty-day expiration date. And . . . wait, where was I?

Oh, yeah! We're talking about something we might call spiritual focus. "Let us keep our eyes fixed on Jesus, on whom our faith depends from beginning to end," says the writer to the Hebrews (Hebrews 12:2, GNT).

Jesus told His followers to "seek first" God's kingdom, even before they thought about what to eat or wear. When we focus on what God wants, He takes care of our needs (Matthew 6:33).

The apostle Paul called Christians to maintain a heavenly perspective:

> Since, then, you have been raised with Christ, set your hearts on things above, where Christ is, seated at the right hand of God. Set your minds on things above, not on earthly things.
> —Colossians 3:1-2

All of these are variations on the lesson learned by Peter on the Sea of Galilee. Stay focused on Jesus. Don't get distracted by the challenges around you.

Stay focused on Jesus. Don't get distracted by the challenges around you.

SWIMMING IN CIRCLES

I learned the importance of focus in a rather embarrassing way.

It was a long-distance swimming event out on a lake. Buoys were set up in a large triangle to mark out the course. We had to swim around the perimeter of this triangle. The total course stretched 1.2 miles.

In my training, I had used a technique of lifting my head on every eighth stroke, so I could see where I was. In that moment, I'd catch sight of the next buoy and make any necessary adjustments to stay on course. But on the day of this event, I had the brilliant idea to try something different. I could save time, I figured, by keeping my head down longer and only lifting it above the water every thirty strokes.

Bad idea. In one of those stretches of thirty strokes, I veered off course, swimming between two buoys. When I lifted my head, I was inside the triangle. I completely lost my bearings and actually began swimming toward a buoy I spotted on the opposite side of the triangle. Fortunately, a judge on a Jet Ski puttered over and said in the nicest possible way, "Hey, idiot, what the heck are you doing?" (or words to that effect). With his help, accompanied by a blatant eye roll in my direction, I got back on the course.

So I learned the practical application of Deuteronomy 5:32 (emphasis added): "So be careful to do what the Lord your God has commanded you; *do not turn aside to the right or to the left.*"

MISSING THE POINT

As we've seen, Jesus challenged His followers to focus and to honor God as the king of their lives and their world. When Jesus preached, God's kingdom was His favorite theme. In story after story, He described how God's kingdom worked. It was full of surprises. God's grace showered down on those who didn't seem to deserve it. The rich and proud and powerful faced God's judgment. More than once, Jesus likened God's kingdom to a party where all sorts of spiritual strugglers were welcome, but the self-righteous refused to attend.

Jesus had a lot of self-righteous people to deal with.

They're known as the Pharisees, members of a sect that controlled the religious culture of the Jews in that time. They were focused on following God's laws, but they were overfocused. They committed themselves to not turning aside to the right or to the left, but they set up unnecessary guard rails (buoys?) to make sure people followed their rules.

Meticulous about following the letter of the law, they ignored the purpose of the law. Once, referring to their practice of measuring out kitchen spices in order to donate the proper percentage, Jesus told them:

> "You give a tenth of your spices—mint, dill and cumin. But you have neglected the more important matters of the law—justice, mercy and faithfulness.... You blind guides! You strain out a gnat but swallow a camel." —Matthew 23:23-24

One of the biggest problems the Pharisees had with Jesus—other than the fact that He often scolded them—was what He did on the Sabbath day. According to the Law, it was supposed to be a day of rest, and religious leaders like the Pharisees had assembled a long list of things people weren't allowed to do on that day. Jesus didn't care about that list. He made a regular practice of healing people on the Sabbath day. This was "work," according to the Pharisees. Forbidden.

Jesus insisted that this restoration was what God intended all along.

RIGIDITY

The Pharisees teach us something important. You can start with a healthy focus and push it to a point of blindness. I'm calling this extreme point "Rigidity." It is the negative extreme of "Focus." Their initial desire to do what God wanted was great, but they soon adopted specific ways to follow God's commands, narrow interpretations of them, and restrictive policies added to the Scriptures.

Ironically, even though the second of the Ten Commandments forbade the crafting of idols that people would worship instead of God, the Pharisees essentially did this with the religious system they crafted. Their rules had become their own idol. Jesus challenged them for this: "You have a fine way of setting aside the commands of God in order to observe your own traditions!" (Mark 7:9).

Once, a Pharisee asked Jesus to name the greatest commandment in God's law. This was probably a trick question. Whatever Jesus chose, He could be accused of neglecting other laws. At first, Jesus played it safe, quoting an overarching command to love the Lord God with your entire self. This was the way many rabbis would answer the question. But then Jesus added a second quotation: "Love your neighbor as yourself" (Matthew 22:39). This, He said, was "like" the command to love God, meaning it was equally important. And He added, "All the Law hang[s] on these two commands" (Matthew 22:40).

This is a crucial insight, and it shows us what the Pharisees got wrong.

Perhaps you know the phrase, "You can't see the forest for the trees." The Pharisees had the commandments in front of them, big pillars of law, like giant tree trunks. But they couldn't see past these trees into the forest of God's love.

Throughout the Gospels, we see the Pharisees judging others (including Jesus) and parading their own piety. Not loving others. While they appeared focused on the intricacies of biblical commands, they actually lost their focus on the loving God who gave those commands. The result was a rigid lifestyle that looked religious but was actually a distortion of what God intended.

We see the same thing today. People find some substitute for God, often something that seems religious, and they harden their lives around that. They fight for it with every ounce of their energy.

They're easily offended by contrary opinions. They condemn those who disagree. But love? Grace? Nowhere to be seen.

BENDING

In one biblical story (see John 8:1-11), the Pharisees brought a woman before Jesus who was caught "in the very act" of adultery. This raises a lot of questions, such as "How did they catch her?" and "What happened to the man?" But put those questions aside and consider the challenge to Jesus.

They were ready to stone her to death, a penalty the Old Testament law established for this crime. Would Jesus affirm this decision?

It was, of course, another trap. If Jesus showed love and forgiveness to the woman, as He often did, they could accuse Him of flouting God's commands.

Jesus stooped down and wrote in the sand with His finger. (Wouldn't you love to know what He wrote? The story doesn't say.) Then He gave a brilliant answer that's now well-known throughout the world, even among those who don't know the Bible well: "Let the one who is without sin cast the first stone" (John 8:9, author paraphrase).

Can you imagine what was going through the minds of this Pharisee gang? I wonder if one of them said, "Theodore, you're the oldest and pretty much the most perfect out of us. You start, and we'll follow!" Theodore quickly remembers the three or four sins he's recently committed but hasn't talked about. So He says, "Um, I would stone her, fellas, but my shoulder's bothering me." So, a few seconds pass, and all the men leave one by one. Jesus tells the woman, "I don't condemn you either. Go now, and stop your sinful ways" (John 8:11, author paraphrase).

FLEXIBLE FOCUS

This is the gospel in a nutshell. Sinners deserve punishment, but we are all sinners. The only person with the moral standing to punish sinners is Jesus, the Son of God, who was "not sent into the world to condemn the world but to save it" (John 3:17). His message of divine love (secured by His sacrificial death) transforms sinners.

Careful! Don't miss this. Let me repeat it. Jesus did not come into the world to condemn the world. So why on earth do people feel like God has called them to condemn the world? Honestly, friends, it's just crazy town out there online. You can go down any number of spiritual rabbit holes and find crowds of so-called Christians hell-bent on condemning others. Haven't they ever read this story?

> *You can go down any number of spiritual rabbit holes online and find crowds of so-called Christians hell-bent on condemning others. Haven't they ever read this story?*

The rigidity of the Pharisees demanded punishment for sin. Jesus responded with what we might call flexibility. He didn't challenge the idea that adultery was sin or that sin should be punished. He kept His focus on the God who gave those commandments and on God's desire for redemption. Jesus found a creative way to humble the proud accusers and offer a new life to the woman.

A HELPFUL, UNTRANSLATABLE WORD

At the end of his letter to the Philippians, Paul gave them a varied collection of advice. Rejoice. Pray. Sort out your spats. But we find a strange word in Philippians 4:5 which could help us in our current discussion.

One translation says to let your "moderation" be known to everyone (KJV). Another translation says let your "reasonableness" be known (ESV). Another says "graciousness" (CSB). Gentleness. Patience.

The Greek word is epieikes, and it's used only a handful of times in the New Testament. As for its meaning, one scholar calls it "one of the truly great Greek words that is almost untranslatable."

Four hundred years before Paul wrote this, Aristotle had a few things to say about this word, contrasting it with the word for justice (dike, dikaios). Like other philosophers, Aristotle was interested in virtue. How could a person live a truly good life? What personal qualities contribute to a healthy society? He used the example of a judge passing sentence on a criminal. A "just" judge would have every right to throw the book at the defendant, but one who practiced epieikes would consider the circumstances. This judge would be reasonable, moderate, even gentle in passing judgment. The goal of justice would still be served but with some flexibility.

Dr. Phil might say, "How's that working for you?" The apostle Paul seems to be saying, "Don't go to the extreme of rigidity. Practice wisdom, gentleness, moderation, and grace in your life, and let others see this."

Perhaps you've seen old newsreel footage of an early suspension bridge that began shaking and ultimately fell apart. It's wild, and it makes the viewer wonder what the builders did wrong.

I'm no architect, but I understand that the bridge was built perfectly. Everything was precisely symmetrical, and that was the problem. When the wind blew, the vibrations bounced back and forth within the structure, doubling back on themselves, creating more and more force that caused the collapse.

It was rigid. It needed flexibility.

When it was rebuilt, the specs were slightly askew, allowing outside pressure to push but then escape. And every suspension bridge built afterward benefited from this colossal fail.

As I understand it, construction in earthquake-prone areas follows the same principle. Skyscrapers are designed to give a little, to bend without breaking.

That's a powerful image for Christians as we feel the tectonic plates of our culture shifting. Rigidity is a recipe for disaster. We need to focus on God's truth but also display the flexibility of grace, gentleness, and moderation. That's how we will build bridges to our neighbors.

Rigidity is a recipe for disaster. We need to focus on God's truth but also display the flexibility of grace, gentleness, and moderation. That's how we will build bridges to our neighbors.

THE OTHER EXTREME

Just as focus can go to the extreme of rigidity, a healthy flexibility can devolve into spinelessness. A spineless person just goes with the flow, not making waves. If God's truth causes problems in a certain situation, or if it's just inconvenient, the "spineless" person dismisses it.

Psalm 1:1-4 (BSB) describes the "blessed" person who finds delight in God's Word, meditating on it "day and night." That person lives a good and fruitful life. By contrast, "the ungodly" have a very different story. The psalm likens them to "chaff driven off by the wind." There's no weight to them, no substance.

The New Testament refers to "double-minded" people who don't turn to God for wisdom. They are "unstable in all they do" (James 1:8). Instability is the inability to stand. They have no backbone. They're jellyfish. An old maxim says, "If you stand for nothing, you'll fall for anything." That's the story of the spineless.

I see this more and more in parenting. I have two teenagers I'm very proud of, but I readily admit I'm no expert. Still, I know that sometimes parents have to say no. It's definitely not the way to win the popularity contest of parenting. "Rocco's parents are letting him go. They don't care what he downloads!"

Well, as parents who do care, we have to say, "As for our house, this is the direction we're going, and Rocco's parents are idiots." We try not to say the "idiot" part out loud—but we've seen how that approach plays out. The spineless parents who "go along to get along" are inadvertently inviting trouble to their dinner table.

But rigidity isn't a winning formula either. Parents who lay down the law and never budge are playing a dangerous game. "My way or the highway" might work while they're under your roof, but

FLEXIBLE FOCUS   43

you're trying to build them into adults who will eventually make wise decisions for themselves. It's also incredibly rewarding when they actually want to come back to see you after their gone. So it's important to strike a balance of the central qualities discussed in this chapter—focus and flexibility. That doesn't mean there won't be any tension in a focused-and-flexible home, but it will be a healthy tension, as the two qualities work in tandem.

BACK TO THE TENSION SPECTRUM

Rigid–Focused–Flexible–Spineless

You see how this spectrum works now, right? There are two qualities in the center that create a healthy tension. You might be more flexible by nature. If so, you might look to develop more focus—or vice versa. But these are both positive qualities that balance each other, like the pole in the hands of a tightrope walker.

Each of these qualities has a negative extreme—in this case, rigidity and spinelessness. If you are naturally more focused, your healthiest move is in the direction of flexibility rather than rigidity. Move toward the center and the healthy tension found there.

As we examine this grid, we find an interesting math to it.

Focused (minus) Flexible = Rigid

Flexible (minus) Focused = Spineless

When you remove the opposite quality in the healthy tension, you create the unhealthy extreme. When the focused person loses all flexibility, it's easy to fall into rigidity. When the flexible person loses focus, they quickly become spineless.

> *When you remove the opposite quality in the healthy tension, you create the unhealthy extreme.*

| Rigid | Focused | | Flexible | Spineless |

Truth   Grace

Here's another observation about the spectrum involving two powerful religious words: Truth and Grace. In fact, several of the healthy tensions in this book could be described as a partnership of truth and grace.

Some people focus on the truth of God—His holiness, His plan, what He wants from people—and they tell others about it. Other people are keenly aware of God's grace—His understanding and forgiveness—and they show that grace to others. These two factors work together as all of us interact with God.

It's interesting that one of the first things the gospel of John says about Jesus is this: "We have seen his glory . . . full of grace and truth" (John 1:14). And as we continue reading the Gospels, we see these qualities played out in Jesus's life and ministry. He courageously speaks the truth of God, even when it's unpopular, but He also offers God's grace to everyone He encounters.

It's tempting to think of grace and truth as opposites, but the fact that Jesus was "full" of both of these qualities would say otherwise. He was 100 percent grace. And 100 percent truth. I've heard it said this way:

Grace without truth is meaningless.
Truth without grace is mean.
Grace and truth together is medicine.

The same is true of focus and flexibility (and the other paired qualities I'll be presenting). They aren't opposites. They complement each other. Both can be part of the wholeness of a Christ-follower. The very goal of finding, valuing, and keeping healthy tension is to live in a way that embodies the convictions, character, and conduct of Christ Himself. With Jesus as our example, we're able to navigate the tensions and become more like Him.

BIBLE HANDLEBARS

How do we steer our way through this grid? Scripture gives us several examples of the combination of focus and flexibility, almost like handlebars on a bike, allowing us to keep our balance as we cycle through life.

Paul's letter to the Galatians looks very much like our grid. In the first few chapters, he attacked a rigid, Pharisee-like group that was forcing the Jewish law on non-Jewish Christians. Then Paul began chapter 5 with a clear plea for freedom and (we might say) flexibility: "So Christ has truly set us free. Now make sure that you stay free, and don't get tied up again in slavery to the law" (verse 1, NLT).

Still, he recognized that flexibility in behavior can lead to a spineless existence. "But don't use your freedom to satisfy your sinful nature." He described the wanton life of those who don't focus on God's Spirit: "sexual immorality, impurity, lustful pleasures, idolatry, sorcery, hostility, quarreling, jealousy, outbursts of anger, selfish ambition, dissension, division, envy, drunkenness, wild parties, and other sins like these" (Galatians 5:13, 19-21, NLT).

By contrast, the Holy Spirit bears positive fruit in the lives of believers: "love, joy, peace, patience, kindness, goodness, faithfulness, gentleness, and self-control" (Galatians 5:22-23, NLT). The apostle ended by exhorting us to "keep in step with the Spirit" (verse 25)—about as clear a definition of focus as we could hope for.

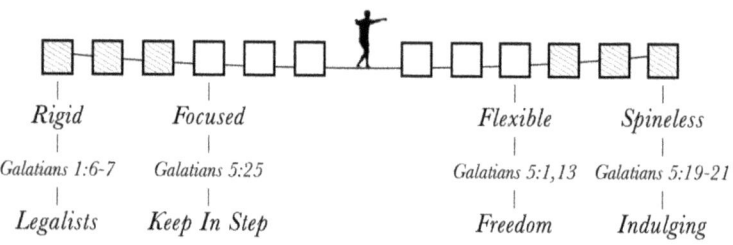

Rigid	Focused	Flexible	Spineless
Galatians 1:6-7	Galatians 5:25	Galatians 5:1,13	Galatians 5:19-21
Legalists	Keep In Step	Freedom	Indulging

We find another extended example in Romans 14, where the apostle Paul discussed "disputable matters" (verse 1). Apparently, some church folks were bickering over what foods were proper to eat or what days should be considered holy.

We don't have to look too far back in modern history to see similar disputes arising over alcohol, card-playing, dancing, length of men's hair, women wearing hats in church, women wearing pants ever, rock music, Smurfs, Halloween, movie-going, etc. I grew up in a pastor's home during the '80s and '90s, so the list could go on and on... and on.

It's oddly comforting to know that similar spats go back two thousand years.

In this masterful chapter, Paul was very flexible, but he was also focused on the well-being of the church. "Therefore let us stop passing judgment on one another. Instead, make up your mind not to put any stumbling block or obstacle in the way of a brother or sister" (Romans 14:13).

Showing flexibility, Paul said it really doesn't matter whether you do this disputed thing or not, but you should be careful not to hurt others. And remember how Jesus told us to "seek first the kingdom"? (See Matthew 6:33, ESV.) That's what Paul did here: "For the kingdom of God is not a matter of eating and drinking, but of righteousness, peace and joy in the Holy Spirit" (Romans 14:17).

Flexibility with focus. Grace and truth in harmony.

> *Flexibility with focus. Grace and truth in harmony.*

PETER ON THE ROOFTOP

I love the larger-than-life example of Simon Peter, the fisherman who accepted an invitation to follow Jesus and start catching people. He could've been the model for some of the roughneck men on *Deadliest Catch*, but he later became a key leader of the Christian movement.

Still, the guy had a knack for saying and doing the wrong thing. We see his growth as we go through the Gospels, and we grow with him, learning more about Jesus on every page. We get to observe several character-defining moments for this man who was just as flawed as we are.

This chapter begins with the tale of Peter's all-too-short stroll on the Sea of Galilee. Let's peek in on him a few years later. Jesus had gone back to heaven. Peter and the other disciples were tending a growing enterprise. People were coming to faith in Jesus, but so far, it had been only Jews, as the young church observed the old laws about avoiding contact with unclean outsiders.

Peter had had a grueling travel schedule, preaching and healing in seacoast towns. Staying with a friend, he went up on the roof before lunch to chill. Literally. In that climate, a flat rooftop was the best place to catch a cool sea breeze.

What Peter didn't realize was that an Italian army officer had been praying in a town not far away. At God's direction, this centurion was sending a squad to bring Peter to his home. He hoped the apostle would tell him about the Jewish God he respected but didn't really know.

On the rooftop, Peter had a vision of animals dancing around like something out of Disney's Fantasia. This wasn't the result of some bad hummus—it was a vision from God. And a voice in the vision said, "Kill and eat" (Acts 10:13).

Peter assumed it was a test of his devotion. These were "unclean" animals, according to the Jewish law. He was not permitted to eat them. He was hungry, yes, but he proudly refused this nonkosher feast: "No way, Yahweh." Peter was sure he would pass God's test. But surprisingly, the voice scolded him: "Do not call something unclean if God has made it clean" (Acts 10:15, NLT).

The vision repeated twice more, and Peter had no clue what it meant—until the soldiers showed up, and the Spirit said very clearly, "Go with them" (Acts 10:20).

Pause a minute and consider what happened here. Was this another keep-your-eyes-on-Jesus moment? Peter thought he was focusing on God's Word, but he came to realize he was actually being rigid. God was doing a new thing in the world, and He wanted Peter on board.

Perhaps Peter thought about all the times Jesus said, "You've heard this, but I say this" (see Matthew 5). He talked about new wine in old wineskins (see Matthew 9). He challenged the rigid party line of the Pharisees and reached across cultural boundaries. Jesus promised to send the Spirit of truth to guide His followers. Was that whom Peter was hearing from now?

Focusing on the Master who kept doing new things, Peter was flexible enough to go and see the Italian officer.

Focusing on the Master who kept doing new things, Peter was flexible enough to go and see the Italian officer. The man and his family came to faith in Jesus, and the world has never been the same.

CHAPTER 3

REAL HOPE

S pies were deployed to scout out the territory before the planned invasion—twelve of them, all well-respected leaders in their communities. The mission: learn about the land, its people, and its defenses.

For more than a month, these agents did their work as the invading force camped at the edge of the desert. Finally, the spies returned, carrying huge clusters of grapes, just some of the bountiful produce of this fertile territory. They said the land was "flowing with milk and honey" (see Numbers 13). After a few years in the desert, this was good news, indeed.

But there was also bad news: "The people who live there are powerful, and the cities are fortified and very large." They had even seen some giant warriors there.

And so a debate began. One of the spies, named Caleb, declared, "We should go up and take possession of the land, for we can certainly do it."

Others replied, "We can't attack those people; they are stronger than we are. The land we explored devours those living in it." They reminded the people that the defenders of the land were huge, members of a giant race. By comparison, they seemed like grasshoppers.

It was an all-night argument. Caleb, now joined by another spy, Joshua, argued, "The land we passed through and explored is exceedingly good. If the Lord is pleased with us, He will lead us into that land, a land flowing with milk and honey, and will give it to us."

The crowd was not buying it. They were turning against these two spies. There was talk of stoning them.

"Do not rebel against the Lord," Caleb pleaded. "And do not be afraid of the people of the land, because we will devour them. Their protection is gone, but the Lord is with us."

Ten spies said, "We can't." Two spies said, "We can." Both groups were right.

> *Ten spies said, "We can't." Two spies said, "We can." Both groups were right.*

Ultimately, the people of Israel refused to invade the land. God forced them to wander through the desert another thirty-eight years, during which time all of the people at that fateful debate died off—except for Caleb and Joshua.

THE REAL REALITY

This story offers a stark comparison between hope and reality. On their fact-finding mission, the twelve spies all experienced the same things. They traveled the same terrain, tasted the same fruit, and felt the same dust beneath their sandals. Yet they came to dramatically different conclusions. Ten said, "There's no way we can do this." Caleb and Joshua said, "There's no way we *shouldn't* do this."

It's customary to criticize the ten spies—and all the Israelites who followed them—for their lack of faith, yet many of us might have stood on that side of the argument. The naysayers weren't entirely wrong. The defenders of Canaan were, indeed, big and strong. The conquest would not be easy. The ten spies who authored the majority report were being realistic. Don't be wowed by the size of the grape clusters. Consider the size of the opposing team!

Jesus Himself said, centuries later, "Suppose a king is about to go to war against another king. Won't he first sit down and consider whether he is able with ten thousand men to oppose the one coming against him with twenty thousand?" (Luke 14:31). That's realism. It's important to know what you're getting into. Scout the opposition. See the full picture.

Yet, as the story of the spies makes clear, there was an important bit of reality that the ten spies—and the whole crowd—were missing. The power of God.

"The Lord is with us!" Caleb contended. As big as the Canaanite giants were, God was bigger. As long as the Israelites were following God's guidance, they were unstoppable. True, any experienced general might look at the scouting report and agree with the majority's no-go decision—but the Israelites had a secret weapon. The Lord was with them.

Apparently, this weapon was so secret that most of the Israelites didn't know they had it.

THE BALLOON AND THE ANCHOR

Long after you've put down this book, I hope you'll remember its key point: seemingly opposing qualities can work together to move us toward spiritual maturity. This chapter sets up "Hopeful" and "Realistic" as the two characteristics with a healthy tension between them. Both hope and realism are good qualities on their own. Together they are even stronger. Yet there are negative extremes on both sides that can do damage.

> *Seemingly opposing qualities can work together to move us toward spiritual maturity.*

I picture hope as a helium balloon. Realism is the anchor that hope is tied to.

Our hopes fly free. They soar into the future. But our sense of what's real keeps those hopes connected to our lives. An untethered balloon is just a pretty dot as it flies into the sky. A string without a balloon is rather pointless. The combination brings joy.

I see this healthy tension in a family from my church. The daughter, Kara, grew up with a severe hearing deficit. She often prayed for healing, and she nurtured a strong belief that it would happen—someday, somehow. Her parents were also committed Christ-followers who fanned her faith into flame while also helping her to be realistic. As they saw it, God can work miracles of healing, but He may often choose a different route. Sometimes, He allows us to go through difficulties for His greater glory.

Kara and her parents lived in the tension between hopeful anticipation for healing and a realistic perspective that supernatural healing may not ever happen. Many in the church benefited from this family's faith and wisdom through this struggle.

At one point, the family had exhausted their options and, after multiple procedures, had come to the conclusion that a specific operation was necessary but would temporarily make Kara completely deaf. This decision was reached shortly before Kara was supposed to go to camp, an experience she always enjoyed.

With her condition worsening and the surgery approaching, Kara wondered if she should even bother attending camp. But she determined to go, despite her insecurity and fear. While at camp, a group of friends gathered around Kara to pray for her. It was not unlike many prayers prayed over her ears before. But in that natural moment, God did the supernatural. Suddenly, Kara could hear. Fully.

Following the service, she called her parents and, with tears trickling down her young face, told them she could hear the cicadas in the night for the first time. Her parents were blown away—but they were also cautious. Would the doctors confirm what their daughter had experienced? When she got home, they immediately took her to their auditory specialist. Clinicians measured her hearing capacity, and the results confirmed what Kara had experienced. She was now scoring not just in a normal range but above average hearing. Now, two years later, her hearing is still above average.

Kara's parents had the wisdom to prepare her for a faithful life, miracle or no miracle. And God was clearly at work, even in the season between the diagnosis and the miracle, in the lives of everyone involved in this story. And Kara herself has learned to recognize the goodness of God in all circumstances: when God fulfills our hopes and when He has a different plan.

Maybe you're in the middle of waiting and waiting until . . . what? Maybe you've been praying for your spouse to come to know Christ. Maybe you've received a difficult diagnosis, and everyone is telling you to have faith, but you're struggling just to hang on. Maybe you're waiting for a new job, a restored relationship, or a much-needed break from your labors. You want to have hope, but you feel like things are hopeless.

I just want to remind you: Jesus meets you right where you are. Keep leaning into Him.

GOING TO EXTREMES: PESSIMISTIC

As mentioned, both of these healthy viewpoints—hopeful and realistic—have extreme variations that are unhealthy. An overdose of a hopeful attitude might be described as *delusional*. On the other side, a realistic attitude can turn into *pessimism*.

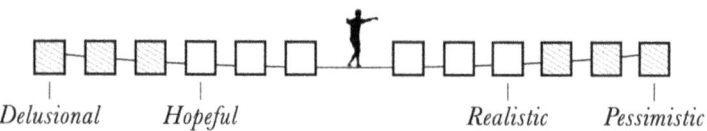

Delusional *Hopeful* *Realistic* *Pessimistic*

The pessimistic extreme goes far beyond reality; it assumes that things will always turn out badly. "Life is hard, and then you die," is often the mantra of people who have suffered great disappointment in life—not just pain and sorrow but disappointment.

I am continually amazed at how well people heal from personal pain. It takes time, but they often come back into a healthy tension of hope and realism. Disappointment is harder to handle because hope has been crushed. People expected one thing and got another. It's very easy for them to assume that life is always like that. Hoping is pointless, they think, because they'll only find more disappointment.

The Bible gives us a glimpse of this mindset in the strange book of Ecclesiastes, written by someone who calls himself the Teacher (in Hebrew, Qoheleth). He has had great wealth, great power, and great accomplishments. All have disappointed him. (Throughout the centuries, many readers have suggested the author was King Solomon.)

The Teacher keeps coming back to the same refrain: "Everything is meaningless!" (Ecclesiastes 1:2 and throughout). Life is just "chasing after the wind" (Ecclesiastes 1:14 and elsewhere). He goes through every activity that might be expected to give life meaning—work, pleasure, fame, wealth, learning—and none of it provides ultimate meaning.

Ecclesiastes is clearly a downer. Like me, you might be wondering, Why is this in the Bible? Does God want us to be so pessimistic?

I believe there's an important clue buried in the Teacher's melancholy. "There is nothing new under the sun," he says (1:9), and later, "My heart began to despair over all my toilsome labor under the sun" (2:20). The phrase "under the sun" appears twenty-seven times. The Teacher's perspective is limited to this world. Without the God who created the sun, nothing else can give real meaning to our lives.

Another Old Testament book also illustrates deep despair, but it takes a different direction. The book of Lamentations is credited to Jeremiah, often called the "weeping prophet." For decades, he called the nation of Judah to get right with God. He warned of impending judgment: God would send the powerful Babylonian army to destroy Jerusalem.

Religious leaders laughed. It was unthinkable that God would let heathens hurt His own temple. They tried to silence the prophet, but it all happened as Jeremiah said. Babylon invaded Jerusalem, plundering the temple and taking many citizens captive. Reading Lamentations, we can almost see the prophet wandering through the ruins of the once-proud city:

He has walled me in so I cannot escape; he has weighed me down with chains. Even when I call out or cry for help, he shuts out my prayer. He has barred my way with blocks of stone; he has made my paths crooked. —Lamentations 3:7-9

As Jeremiah mourned the punishment the Lord had sent, he reflected the deep feelings of disappointment and despair that lead many into a permanent pessimism: "I have been deprived of peace; I have forgotten what prosperity is" (Lamentations 3:17).

But then his mood changed:

Yet this I call to mind and therefore I have hope: Because of the Lord's great love we are not consumed, for his compassions never fail. They are new every morning; great is your faithfulness. —Lamentations 3:21-23

The prophet rediscovered hope, and while his circumstances remained dire, he recognized that the Lord's love was also part of his reality.

THE SUBTRACTION PRINCIPLE

In our last chapter—exploring the healthy tension between being Focused and Flexible—we observed an almost mathematical principle about the extremes. The extreme characteristic appears when one of the two parts of the healthy tension is removed:
› To be Flexible and not Focused makes you Spineless.
› To be Focused and not Flexible yields Rigid behavior.

Here, we find the same principle at work.
› To be Realistic and not Hopeful makes you Pessimistic.
› To be Hopeful and not Realistic yields Delusional thinking.

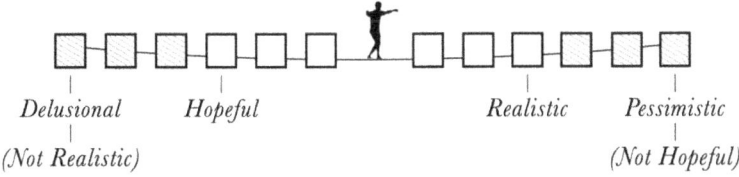

Delusional　　*Hopeful*　　　　　*Realistic*　　*Pessimistic*
(Not Realistic)　　　　　　　　　　　　　　*(Not Hopeful)*

The way to avoid the unhealthy extremes is to keep the two central qualities in balance. If you are both realistic and hopeful, you will stay out of the danger zones.

The way to avoid the unhealthy extremes is to keep the two central qualities in balance.

GOING TO EXTREMES: DELUSIONAL

Optimism sells sneakers.

How many middle-aged couch potatoes shell out way too much for a pair of Nikes because they are definitely going to start working out this time? Hope overrides realism.

There's a reason that Christian athletes don't put references from Leviticus on their eye black. The scripture stenciled under Tim Tebow's lashes wasn't "I only eat split-hoof animals" (see Leviticus 11:3). No, it was "Phil. 4:13," a far more inspirational choice: "I can do all things through Christ who strengthens me (NKJV)."

We want Jeremiah 29:11 on the graduation cards we send—"I know the plans I have for you . . . a future with hope" (author paraphrase)—and not "It is appointed unto men once to die, but after this the judgment" (Hebrews 9:27, KJV).

We like optimism, and that's not a bad thing. But when the helium balloon of hope shakes off the anchor of reality, it ends up out of reach and out of sight.

"Delusional" optimism is especially a problem among Christians. This is not just hope in the power of God to do amazing things. It's denial that anything could go wrong. In many cases, it puts a burden on believers. "If only you had more faith, the storerooms of heaven would open to you, and you'd be wealthy, healthy, successful, and popular. But apparently your faith is weak."

This is a twisted view of the promises of God. As Joshua and Caleb said in Numbers 14:9, "The Lord is with us," and great things can indeed happen in His strength, according to His plans. We can hope and pray for positive outcomes, but we also recognize that God's ways are higher than our ways (see Isaiah 55:9), and sometimes He leads us on the paths we don't prefer.

Yes, the Bible says, "Rejoice in the Lord always" (Philippians 4:4), but it also says, "Weep with those who weep" (Romans 12:15, NLT) and "Blessed are those who mourn" (Matthew 5:4). Hey, I like joy. It is part of our reality as children of God, but so is sorrow. Jesus wept. And if He wept, so can we. In fact, we have the whole gamut of human emotion at our disposal.

ACCEPTING THE REALITY OF GRIEF

My sister-in-law was a saint. A deeply committed Christ-follower and also a devoted servant of God, Jamie had a special calling on her life and would become a missionary. While on assignment in northern Asia, she was diagnosed with breast cancer, already quite far along. Our family prayed fervently. Our church prayed. We amassed an international army of prayer warriors to pound on heaven's doors. We believed that God could work a miracle and stop this disease in its tracks. Imagine the power of that testimony: people on two continents would see the power and love of God. How could this miracle *not* happen? If anyone deserved to be healed, it was this faithful missionary. Strategically, from our perspective, it made no sense for God to take her at such a young age, leaving behind two children under five.

And yet He did.

We wept. We mourned. We walked around in a daze for a while. Well-meaning but incredibly insensitive Christians would approach my wife (Jamie's sister) and say, "All things work together for good," or, "If Jamie would've just gone to this natural doctor or started taking this green drink or that extract. . . ." I had to keep my wife from pouncing on them like a puma. In that time, my family didn't need an herbal remedy or even a theology lesson. We really just needed people to sit with us in our sorrow.

The Bible offers comfort to those in sorrow. The apostle Paul gave one church a glimpse of Christ's return: "So you will not grieve like people who have no hope" (1 Thessalonians 4:13, NLT). As members of God's family, we have hope, but we still grieve when we suffer loss. Our hope is not in the power of our faith to prevent anything bad from happening. We put our hope in God whose love and grace and purpose will prevail.

WHAT HOPE CAN SEE

I've enjoyed watching the Tolkien-inspired TV series *The Rings of Power*. Like Tolkien's *Lord of the Rings* trilogy, it presents epic struggles between forces of good and evil. In one exchange, someone mentions that the king's plans are resting on mere hope. The king replies: "Hope is never mere, even when it is meager. When all the other senses sleep, the eye of hope is first to awaken, last to shut."

I've been mulling over that for months now. The reference to "the eye of hope" is brilliant because hope is largely about vision. What's your view of the future? Do you see a way out of the current mess? What kind of larger plan do you picture?

As Christians, we see a reality with God in it.

Once, while reading a line about an "eternal optimist," I twisted the words into "eternal optometrist." That's actually not bad. Instead of creating some delusional world in which nothing bad ever happens, we can check our hopeful vision against reality and also recognize the eternal aspect of that reality.

> *Instead of creating some delusional world in which nothing bad ever happens, we can check our hopeful vision against reality and also recognize the eternal aspect of that reality.*

The Lord is with us! That's how Caleb saw the future of Israel, though others didn't share his vision. The Lord is with us! That fact filters the way we see the world, everything we experience, and all we expect in the future. As pioneer missionary William Carey said, we can "attempt great things for God; expect great things from God"—not because we're guaranteed success but because we're confident that God is at work in our world. The Lord is with us! We can't know for sure that everything will go swimmingly, but we can be assured that we are swimming in the ocean of God's eternal purpose.

Our old friend, Qoheleth the Teacher, as pessimistic as he was, wrote that God "has planted eternity in the human heart, but even so, people cannot see the whole scope of God's work from beginning to end" (Ecclesiastes 4:13, NLT). Yes, we can be eternal optometrists, scanning a future horizon that extends into eternity, but we're still learning about what God's up to. Hope is never mere—minor, trivial—even when it is meager. Yes, we will go through difficult times when our hopes are faint, but we put our hope in a powerful God. That's the reality we live in.

CHAPTER 4

HUMBLY CONFIDENT

I feel small.

Throughout my childhood, I was small. A fizzled-out pituitary gland created a growth-hormone deficiency that not only caused complete blindness in one eye but also drastically stunted my physical development. In sixth grade, I weighed seventy pounds and stood 3'6". Add to that a left blind eye that had a wandering mind of its own, and you get the picture: I was super short and a little cross-eyed. "Ladykiller" was not my nickname, I assure you.

As kids collect fireflies in a jar, as they amass bumps and bruises and scars from playing on playgrounds, they begin gathering, inch by inch, their sense of self-worth. And, face it, in our formative years, there's great value placed on how we look and how we perform. In this department, I had major self-image obstacles to overcome.

> *Insecurity can become either quicksand or jet fuel.*

Insecurity can become either quicksand or jet fuel. I experienced both. That feeling of smallness continues to plague me, even as I've grown to reasonable adult proportions. I easily sink into the quicksand of self-doubt. (Even as I'm writing this chapter, there's an internal dialogue that propels and terrifies me simultaneously. Will this make sense? Do I really have anything valuable to add to this conversation? Am I just complaining here or wanting to garner sympathy?)

However, my childhood insecurity has also propelled me to prove myself in various ways. As a kid, I strove to be the funniest in class, often poking fun at myself. I knew I'd never be the biggest, but I could be the fastest, motoring those little legs to outpace the big guys. Even now, my interest in the Iron Man competition is supposed to be driven by a desire to stay healthy and active, but in reality, I think it's also my own grown-up attempt to win a childhood battle.

Maybe you can relate.

People everywhere are still dealing with schoolyard taunts and youthful rejections. Insecurity drags them down or shoots them forward—sometimes both at the same time. No matter how high you rise in your profession, you might still succumb to the nagging fear that you're not up to the task.

THE SPECTRUM

As we build our collection of healthy tensions, we come to the attributes of confidence and humility. These people are "Confident" and

"Humble." These two seemingly opposite characteristics can actually work together to solidify a positive sense of identity. Before we explore that tension, let's consider the outer edges of our grid, the extremes.

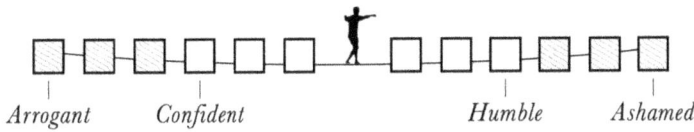

Arrogant   *Confident*   *Humble*   *Ashamed*

Already we've examined the "I feel small" mindset. This goes beyond feeling humble; it's feeling insecure or even ashamed of who you are. It's more than the temporary shame over something you've done wrong—something that can be confessed and forgiven. No, this shame is rooted in your understanding of who you are. This "Ashamed" person senses that he or she has no value.

"But I am a worm and not a person, a disgrace of mankind and despised by the people," a psalmist wrote in the midst of soul-shattering rejection (Psalm 22:6, NASB). Within this worm mentality, people feel they have nothing to offer society. Even those closest to them—family, friends, colleagues—would be better off without them. This also affects their relationship with God. That same psalm begins with the phrase Jesus quoted on the cross: "My God, my God, why have you forsaken me?"

I have deep compassion for people who feel this way. I've been there. For those at clinical levels of low self-esteem, I strive to actively advocate to our church body, my friends, and my fellow pastors the importance of seeking professional counseling in order to rebuild a healthy, Christ-centered sense of identity.

Yet sometimes, Christians think they're supposed to wallow in shame. They start with a base of total depravity, stir in some "Sinners in the Hands of an Angry God," and sprinkle some worm references on top, and they feast on shame sushi. They routinely refuse to serve in any capacity at church because they feel they have no talents worth giving to God. They constantly put others first—which is wonderful—except they keep reminding everyone else that they're doing so.

I know of one woman who would sneak out of her church's evangelistic services during the altar call, so her sinful presence wouldn't keep the Spirit from working. This might seem like a selfless attitude, but it's actually immensely self-centered, not to mention incredibly misguided. Would God actually refrain from saving people because she was in the room? Of course not!

Scripture urges us to be humble, but it also encourages confidence in what God is doing in our lives. Abject shame dismisses that confidence and takes humility to an unhealthy level.

ARROGANCE

One of the most beautiful moments in a young person's life is when a parent says, "I'm proud of you." That's a good kind of pride.

It can also be good when people of any age try something new, do something good, or use their abilities to help others. They might say, "I'm proud of myself for doing that." That can also be a good kind of pride, a satisfaction in contributing to a good outcome. I went skydiving on my birthday to attempt to tackle a fear and show my kids I was willing to do something daring. Immediately after landing in the field below, I threw up. Everywhere. Whether from dizziness or abject fear, my body decided to expel all the contents of my stomach and then some. So I'm not sure if my kids were proud of me or not! But I was! I was so proud that I decided I never have to do that again. Ever!

> *When a healthy pride gets just a lace of arrogance mixed in, it creates a dangerous extreme.*

But here's the poison. When a healthy pride gets just a lace of arrogance mixed in, it creates a dangerous extreme.

"Arrogant" people consider themselves more important than others, more talented, more attractive, or just, well, better. Their world revolves around them. They find it nearly impossible to accept defeat. They seldom respect the opinions of others. If they show kindness, it's probably a ploy to get something in return.

Arrogant people love to display evidence of their superiority, and so they keep bringing up the elite college they attended, they insist on being called Doctor, or they drive a top-of-the-line car whether they can afford it or not. They're name-droppers. If they have a position of authority, they love giving orders to underlings. They love to correct your grammar.

An oft-quoted proverb says, "Pride goes before destruction, a haughty spirit before a fall" (Proverbs 16:18). It's clearly talking about more than simple satisfaction in a job well done, but about the "haughty spirit" of arrogance. A high and mighty attitude. Why does it lead to a fall? Because it's not based on anything true or substantial. The world does not revolve around these people. No matter how smart or gifted they are, they need the people around them. When they overestimate their own value, they make bad decisions. Arrogance has led to disastrous business deals, unwise investments, broken families, and a great deal of loneliness—not to mention the spiritual issues involved in refusing to bow before the Creator.

You might think that arrogance would be absent from the church. After all, didn't Jesus bless the "poor in spirit," welcome children, and warn against "exalting yourself"? Yes, yes, and yes, but we still have arrogance in our ranks. In fact, Christianity provides a new arena in which people can parade their superiority. Many see themselves as more righteous than other churchgoers or more theologically astute. No one is immune to the plague of pride, arrogance, and self-centered ambition.

Jesus's disciples often jockeyed for position, arguing about who was the greatest. James and John, who already seemed to be (with Peter) in the Top Three, lobbied for leading roles in the government Jesus was setting up. He often talked about the kingdom of God; perhaps, they could serve together as prime ministers. In one of the Gospels, their mother came to Jesus with this request. The Master warned them that such honor only came through suffering. Were they ready to suffer with Jesus?

This encounter created a teaching moment for all the disciples and for us. Jesus wanted to differentiate between God's way and the world's way:

> *"You know that those who are regarded as rulers of the Gentiles lord it over them, and their high officials exercise authority over them. Not so with you. Instead, whoever wants to become great among you must be your servant, and whoever wants to be first must be slave of all."* —Mark 10:42-44

These verses should be engraved on the arches of every seminary. They should be read at every church board meeting. Yes, the world rewards arrogance. Sometimes it seems that society is run by people who are full of themselves. But, as Jesus said, "Not so with you" (Mark 10:43). As followers of a Savior who humbled Himself, we must take the low road—the road of sacrificial service, not self-promotion.

THE CIRCLE

By now, we're familiar with the pattern, right? Two qualities exist in a healthy tension. On both sides, there are extremes to be avoided. In this case, I would ask the confident person to lean toward humility rather than arrogance. I would ask the humble person to lean toward confidence rather than shame.

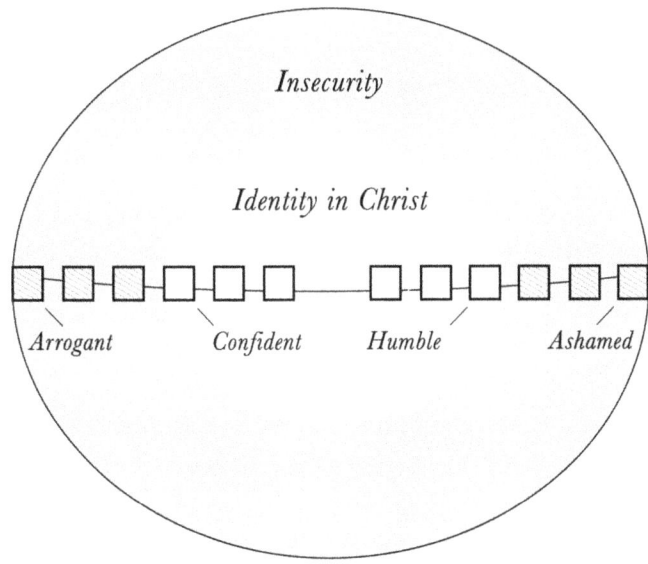

But here's the curious thing about this grid. The extremes are not completely different from each other. Both the arrogant person and the ashamed person can be focused on themselves. Both can be driven by insecurity about who they are and why they exist. While the arrogant may go to great lengths to prove their superiority (perhaps even to themselves), the ashamed may fret that their inferiority will drag down those around them.

The main difference between the healthy center of this spectrum and the unhealthy extremes is that those in the center know who they are. Healthy, humble people know their limitations and are happy to help others. Confident people have a healthy sense of purpose and a realistic view of their strengths. Spiritually speaking, both the confident and humble understand their identity as beloved children whom God has called and gifted to serve His purposes.

> *Spiritually speaking, both the confident and humble understand their identity as beloved children whom God has called and gifted to serve His purposes.*

BOOK IT

As you might expect, there are many Bible passages about humility, but Scripture also gives us good reasons for confidence. The theme verse for this chapter might be Romans 12:3 (CSB):

> For by the grace given to me, I tell everyone among you not to think of himself more highly than he should think. Instead, think sensibly, as God has distributed a measure of faith to each one.

Think about that. There's a certain level of self-appreciation that you "should" have. It could be described as modest, reasonable or moderate, or even sane. That level of confidence is good and right, but don't think of yourself more highly than that. This is exactly the difference between confidence and arrogance that we've been considering.

Romans 12:6-8 goes on to talk about the abilities God gives us—and tells us to use them: "If your gift is . . . serving, then serve; if it is teaching, then teach" (verse 7). We haven't acquired these talents on our own; they are gifts from God. Yet it would be a mistake to bury these talents, to refuse to acknowledge these abilities out of some overwrought humility. "Oh, I couldn't possibly teach that Bible study," might sound like you're being humble, but it crosses the line into being inappropriately ashamed. If your gift is teaching, then teach. Scripture could not be clearer.

The biblical call to confidence starts early, in the first chapter, where we learn that "God created mankind in his own image, in the image of God he created them; male and female he created them" (Genesis 1:27). What does it mean to be made in God's image? I've read many theories about that, and I'm not going to sort through them all here. The essential truth is that God put humans at the pinnacle of creation, made us to resemble Him in some way, and gave us the ability to "rule" the earth. Does that sound like a "worm" to you? Of course not! We are not worms. We are image-bearers of the God of the universe!

A psalmist expounds on this:
You have made them [humans] a little lower than the angels and crowned them with glory and honor. You made them rulers over the works of your hands; you put everything under their feet. —Psalm 8:5-6

At the end of one of the most dramatic chapters in the Bible, Romans 8, Paul lists a number of hardships faced by followers of Jesus in the first century (and beyond) but concludes, "In all these things we are more than conquerors through him who loved us" (Romans 8:37).

Are you seeing the pattern here? We can have great confidence—but not in ourselves. We trust the power of God to work in and through us. I'd love for you to memorize this verse, which sets forth that idea in crystal-clear fashion: "I am sure of this, that he who started a good work in you will carry it on to completion until the day of Christ Jesus" (Philippians 1:6, CSB).

HUMBLE BRAGS IN REVERSE

Maybe you know about "humble bragging." Folks on social media love to identify such statements from people trying to seem humble while puffing up their own reputation. "I was so nervous when I accepted my Book of the Year award, I must have sounded like an idiot." Yes, it's a self-effacing comment, but I did manage to tell you about my award. (And I hope you realize I just made that up. I have not won any such award . . . yet.)

There's a growing number of examples of these humble-not-humble comments:

> - "I'm wearing a ponytail, rolled out of bed from a nap, at the bar with my guy and guys are still hitting on me. Like really?" (Ames Lorraine)
> - "Can we start a media campaign to question how I got into Columbia...still scratching my head..." (Annie Duke)
> - "I just stepped on gum. Who spits gum on a red carpet?" (Carolyn Fell)

The humble brag is a mash-up of confidence and humility, but it's not rooted in reality. The braggers want to seem like they don't feel worthy of attention, acceptance, or an appearance on the red carpet, but they also want to broadcast that they are worthy of all that. They might be trying to sound endearingly self-effacing, but they come across as phony.

When Scripture portrays confidence and humility, it's not humble bragging but a deep synthesis of the two. We are humble before God, and yet we are confident in God.

"We are the clay, you are the potter," prayed the prophet Isaiah, "we are all the work of your hand" (Isaiah 64:8). If we have anything to brag about, it came from the Creator who molded us.

The apostle Paul picks up that theme. While making it abundantly clear that we are saved by God's grace and not by our own righteous works, he added, "We are God's handiwork, created in Christ Jesus to do good works, which God prepared in advance for us to do" (Ephesians 2:10).

The Greek word for "handiwork" is poiema. You can see the word "poem" in there, but it can refer to any work of art. We are God's masterpiece, we might say, but it's clear that He's the artist, not us. It is God's work and not our own, that saves, equips, and empowers us.

This is a recurring theme in Scripture—not the humble brag but confident humility.

This is a recurring theme in Scripture—not the humble brag but confident humility.

Again and again, God has chosen unlikely heroes and worked mightily through them. The great accomplishments happen "not by might nor by power," the Lord says, "but by my Spirit" (Zechariah 4:6).

"God chose the lowly things of this world and the despised things—and the things that are not—to nullify the things that are, so that no one may boast before him" (1 Corinthians 1:28-29). If you're picking teams for, say, a volleyball match, you want the strongest, quickest, most athletic players, right? But God does things differently. He wants the lowly and despised players on His team—so everyone will know that the victory comes from God.

Let me be honest with you: pastors are often tempted by pride. It's easy to start bragging about the size of our churches, the number of campuses we lead, or the magnitude of our multimedia platform. Look at all these great things we're doing for God! But the biblical reality is exactly the reverse. Not a single accomplishment, statistic, or leadership trait comes from us. We are simply lowly people who have been chosen by God to do great things!

There's no place for boasting. We rejoice whenever we participate in the great work of God, but we know it's all His doing. Our humility is not a show—not a humble brag meant to impress others—but a recognition of the simple truth of the matter.

We can be confident that God created us purposefully and joyfully, that He loves us deeply, and that He works through us powerfully. Yet we are humble servants. As we keep those two realities in our minds and hearts, we find a healthy tension.

"Humble yourselves before the Lord, and he will lift you up" (James 4:10).

TWO KINGS

The first two kings of Israel give us intriguing examples of the qualities we've been considering.

Saul was "as handsome a young man as could be found anywhere in Israel, and he was a head taller than anyone else" (1 Samuel 9:2). When we first meet tall Saul, he's on an errand for his father, searching for runaway donkeys. He seeks the help of the prophet Samuel.

Unbeknownst to him, the Lord had just told Samuel that it was time to anoint a king to unify the Israelite tribes. (Really, this was God's concession to His people's relentless nagging for a human king rather than serving God as their one true king. But that's another story.) When Saul showed up, Samuel knew he was the one.

"Why do you say such a thing to me?" the young man protested.

He was from a small family in a small tribe—certainly not royal material.

We find two chapters of festivities involved in the anointing and coronation of Saul. At one point, he stopped in his hometown, and a relative asked where he's been.

"Looking for the donkeys," Saul humbly replied. No word of the anointing.

Later, when all the tribes had gathered and it was time to crown him, Saul couldn't be found. He was hiding among the baggage.

It's always risky to analyze the psychology of Bible characters, but Saul gives us a lot to work with. While the events of his accession to the throne may display an endearing humility, there might be a deeper issue. I suspect that this is an example of the extreme state we've identified as Ashamed.

Saul proved to be a great soldier and an effective general for a time, yet a volatile leader for the nation. It was a pivotal time for Israel as the Philistines were pressing eastward from the sea with superior weaponry, and other neighboring nations were launching occasional raids. Saul's military prowess kept Israel intact for about twenty years.

Well, actually it was the power of God working through the military prowess of Saul and others. But it's not always clear that Saul understood that. It seems that a growing arrogance was taking hold of him. On one wartime afternoon, Saul grew weary of waiting for Samuel, the prophet-priest, to arrive and offer a prebattle sacrifice, so he performed the sacrifice himself. On another occasion, he disobeyed God's explicit instructions, leading to God's rejection of Saul as king and provoking Samuel's great principle: "To obey is better than sacrifice" (1 Samuel 15:22).

Then the shepherd boy arrived.

David was just delivering sandwiches to his brothers who were serving in Saul's army. The Philistine giant Goliath was taunting the Israelites and their God, and little David felt he had to respond. His answer to Goliath was full of confidence, but it was confidence in the Lord:

> *"All those gathered here will know that it is not by sword or spear that the Lord saves; for the battle is the Lord's, and he will give all of you into our hands."* —1 Samuel 17:47

You know the story. The shepherd with the slingshot slayed the giant, and the enemy scattered. David became a national hero, and Saul hailed him as such, essentially welcoming him into the royal family—at least until the king tried to kill the boy wonder.

HUMBLY CONFIDENT

Some scholars would say Saul exhibited signs of bipolar disorder. Consumed by jealousy, he raged against young David, and then he was effusively repentant. He chased David and his squadron through the caverns of the Judean Desert. On a few occasions, the giant slayer had opportunity to sneak up on the king and kill him, but he refused. As long as Saul was king, it was up to God whether he lived or died.

It is possible to see King Saul bouncing madly around the circle of Insecurity—Arrogant one day and Ashamed the next. Meanwhile, David showed both confidence in the Lord's leading and humility about his own status. He knew who he was—and who he was not.

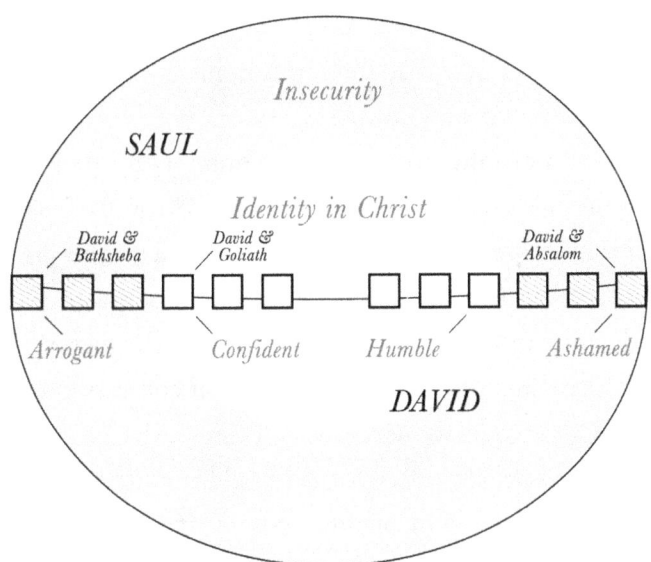

SLIPPAGE

David ascended the throne shortly after Saul's humiliating death in battle against the Philistines. David was not a perfect king or a perfect man. Though he was greatly praised as a first-rate military leader, rallying the nation of Israel behind him even before he wore the crown, he allowed his own dysfunctions to develop major family problems, and these caused rebellion in his home and seasons of incredible difficulty for the nation.

There was also one grievous sin, first private, then very public, which we might consider a major slide into arrogance. With his army off at war, from the heights of his palace, the king saw a woman he wanted—and he took her. After all, he was king. It doesn't matter that she was married, that she was married to a soldier, or that this soldier was part of David's loyal squadron. A king gets what he wants.

After arranging the death of her husband in battle, he gallantly took the widowed Bathsheba as his own queen. His confidence in the Lord was now morphed into pride in his own position.

And he almost got away with it.

God sent a prophet to reintroduce humility to the king's life. David responded with contrition and deep sorrow for his actions. I never want to take David's sin lightly. It was a terrible crime. He didn't get a pass just because he wrote some good songs.

And yet he did write some good songs. In the mercy of God, Psalm 51, credited to David as his prayer of confession over this sin, serves as a model for us today:

> You do not delight in sacrifice, or I would bring it; you do not take pleasure in burnt offerings. My sacrifice, O God, is a broken spirit; a broken and contrite heart you, God, will not despise. —Psalm 51:16-17

Any of us can slide into arrogance when we forget that we owe everything we are to God. Any of us can slide into shame when we forget that we are God's masterpieces, loved and empowered by Him. Let's stay in that healthy tension.

In his second letter to the Corinthians, Paul gives us a great perspective for walking in confident humility:

> *We are confident of all this because of our great trust in God through Christ. It is not that we think we are qualified to do anything on our own. Our qualification comes from God.*
> —*2 Corinthians 3:4-5 (NLT)*

CHAPTER 5

CANDID AND KIND

It was a surprising conversation.

A Jewish rabbi and a Samaritan divorcee broke several cultural taboos when they happened to meet under the noonday sun at a historic watering hole. For one thing, there were centuries of bad blood between Jews and Samaritans, some stemming from historical alliances and past atrocities, but it was also a religious conflict. As Jews saw it, the Samaritans had a hybrid faith, dangerously mixing truth and error.

Besides that, for any man to converse with any unrelated woman would be on the edge of scandal—add in a questionable sexual history, and you've got cover-story material for the Jerusalem Enquirer. You would expect a well-regarded rabbi to be more careful, no matter how thirsty He was.

One more surprise: He had sent His entourage into town, almost as if He wanted to have an unchaperoned conversation with this woman.

The conversation itself, recorded in John 4:1-26 (author paraphrase), revealed a remarkable exchange of candor and kindness. This might be the greatest surprise of all—not only that Jesus had this conversation but that He communicated such divine love through it.

"Please give me a drink," He said. She seemed stunned that He crossed the cultural boundaries to speak with her. Then, He offered her "living water."

"But sir," she replied, "you don't have a rope or a bucket, and this well is very deep. Where would you get this living water? And besides, do you think you're greater than our ancestor Jacob, who gave us this well?"

It's unclear whether she was genuinely curious or picking a fight.

Jesus told her more about this living water, how it "becomes a fresh, bubbling spring" within a person, providing "eternal life."

"Give me this water!" she exclaimed. Again, we're not sure if this is budding faith or jaded mockery.

So far, it has been fairly easy for Jesus to be both candid and kind. Just by speaking to her, He had shown kindness, and He had been quite honest about what He had to offer. But now the conversation needed to find a new level.

"Go and get your husband," said Jesus.

"I don't have a husband," the woman replied.

This is where things escalated. "You're right!" Jesus said. "You don't have a husband—for you have had five husbands, and you aren't even married to the man you're living with now. You certainly spoke the truth!"

If she were mocking Him earlier, He might be responding in kind. He knew her checkered past, and He was still talking with her. We often see her situation through a modern American lens, assuming she had had affairs and left her five husbands. But it's far more likely that some husbands died, others rejected her, and her current man was using her without giving her the rights of a wife. This is probably not a story of wantonness but victimhood. She probably felt that she was damaged goods, worthless to everyone, including God. In that context, the kindness of Jesus was sorely needed. But His candor is important too. He cut through her cover story by saying, in essence, I see who you really are, and I still offer you living water.

This was the moment she realized He was someone special.

"Sir," she said, "you must be a prophet."

Then she asked Him a theological question—but not a trivial one. It goes to the heart of the conflict between Jews and Samaritans. Where is the right place to worship?

As He did so often, Jesus answered a different question. She asked where; He answered Who. "The God of spirit and truth is worshiped in spirit and truth—whether on your mountain or in our temple." Do you know Him?

We see spirit and truth in Jesus's behavior in this encounter and throughout the Gospels. With this woman, He exuded a spirit of kindness along with a command of the truth. When she wondered aloud whether He might be the promised Messiah, He told the truth again: "I Am."

SPEAKING THE TRUTH IN LOVE

In this chapter, we focus on two very good qualities: being "Candid" and being "Kind." Nearly everyone would agree that both are very important. They are among the first things we teach our kids, right? Be nice, and tell the truth. Yet it's surprising how often we find it difficult to do both at the same time.

Jesus made it look so easy, but we struggle with it. I know I do. I have this uncanny ability to deliver the truth without love to those I love the most.

Say a friend of yours gets a haircut and asks what you think of it. In all honesty, it looks hideous to you. Do you say that? Most of us have learned not to if we want to keep that friendship. But should we lie and say we love it? That doesn't seem right either. We may bow out with statements like, "I'm not a hair expert," or "I don't think that style would look good on me." These statements merely avoid the question. They aren't helpful to our friend or their new do. What the friend needs in this moment is honesty presented in a kind, helpful way from someone they trust. (In other words, they need the truth about their hair from someone who really cares.)

I never said these healthy tensions would be easy.

> *I never said these healthy tensions would be easy.*

On both sides, there are extremes. If you stop telling the hard truth to people, you'll just be flattering. If you stop showing love, you become overly critical. Chances are, you know people at both of those extremes. If so, you've probably stopped asking their opinion. You know the flatterer won't tell you the truth, and the critic will hurt your feelings. You turn to the folks who balance candor and kindness.

The apostle Paul wasn't talking about hairstyles when he coined the helpful phrase "speaking the truth in love" (Ephesians 4:15). He was talking about spiritual maturity. Early in that chapter, he said: "Be completely humble and gentle; be patient, bearing with one another in love. Make every effort to keep the unity of the Spirit through the bond of peace" (Ephesians 4:2-3).

Do you see the hard words there? There's "effort" involved. You'll have to "be patient" with some people, "bearing with" them. This is the candid truth. The unity of the church is not all casseroles and kumbaya. Often, we get on one another's nerves.

That's why God has given some people leadership gifts to help people meet these challenges in mature ways:

Then we will no longer be infants, tossed back and forth by the waves, and blown here and there by every wind of teaching and by the cunning and craftiness of people in their deceitful scheming. —Ephesians 4:14

Here we meet the flatterers. "Flattering" people are cunning, crafty, and deceitful schemers who tell people whatever they want to hear, taking advantage of their immaturity. They may seem to be full of kindness, but there is no truth in them.

"Instead, speaking the truth in love, we will grow," Paul says (Ephesians 4:15). Together, with our different personalities, preferences, and abilities, we will learn to function together, just like a human body with its different parts. By telling the truth and showing Christ-like love, we will learn to deal with those who annoy us.

When we put all this together, our spectrum looks like this:

Once again, we find the Christ-like qualities of grace and truth in the center. The kind person shows grace in relationships, always thinking and speaking the best about others. The candid person sees the truth and speaks it, even when it might be unpopular or unwelcome. When candor and kindness—truth and grace—fuse together in a healthy tension, we find spiritual maturity. The candid person genuinely tries to help others by presenting the truth. The kind person tries to support others in truthful ways rather than empty flattery.

The subtraction principle, which we've seen in previous "healthy tensions," applies here too. Remove kindness, and the candid person becomes a "Critical" person, telling the hard truth in a harsh way. Subtract honest candor, and the kind person easily becomes flattering, telling any lie the person wants to hear.

THE SPIRIT OF CRITICISM

In the word itself, you can hear the serpent's hiss. Criti-ssssizzzz-m. It's a sneaky, snaky way to live.

The tempter tears us down at every opportunity and gets us to tear others down. Criticism is contagious. One whiff, and we contract the plague without even realizing it. It causes:

› Blind spots where we don't see our own failings.
› Deaf spots when we don't hear how critical we sound.
› Dumb spots where we pontificate on matters we know nothing about.
› Hot spots where we just spout off, fly off the handle, and lash out irrationally because we just want to gnaw away at something.

When we find ourselves on the receiving end of criticism, we often try to build ourselves back up by criticizing others. That never really works though. A critical spirit can quickly take over a whole group, a family, a marriage, or a church.

A friend recently told me about his high school days:

A new guy started hanging around my group of friends. He was smart, likable, and talented—but his main talent was making up insults. With wit and humor, he criticized everybody else in that group. And here's the strangest thing: instead of turning people against him, it made him more popular. We all kept trying to deliver insults that were as clever as his.

That story comes from fifty years ago, but I've seen the same thing in generation after generation since then. For some people, it's just a phase they eventually grow out of. At a certain point, they realize how impossible it is to build yourself up by tearing others down, and they soften their spirit. But too many of us get stuck there, living our lives with an unchecked, critical, and cynical outlook. And it is highly addictive.

A few years ago, I had a guy in our church (we'll call him Les because that is his name) who was incredibly critical of my leadership, my preaching, the direction of the church, my hairstyle, how much I ate Chick-fil-A (not kidding)—you name it, he was critical of it. However, the more he criticized me, the more I became critical of him. The more he gouged me with random insults, the more I dwelt on what I was going to say to him the next time he spouted off nonsense. Strangely enough, the very thing that fired me up about him, I was learning from him.

Criticism is a highly infectious disease that can attack any person at any time, the more we dwell on it and consume it.

Criticism is a highly infectious disease that can attack any person at any time.

It often stems from insecurity. In many cases, a person who has received regular criticism tries to even the score by lashing out at others. Some critics tell themselves they are upholding standards. In the arts, professional critics pounce on any subpar performance. In the church, we often have amateur critics second-guessing the behavior of others. And I often hear people challenging my theology.

They usually think they're helping. As they see it, they're speaking an inconvenient but necessary truth into the situation. But there's a huge difference between building up and tearing down. I appreciate the truth-tellers in my life. Sometimes they say things that are hard to hear, yet I know they are speaking the truth in love. Not so with those who are consumed by a critical spirit. They enjoy the feeling of superiority they get from pointing out my failings.

CANDID AND KIND

Jesus said, "Do not judge, or you too will be judged" (Matthew 7:1). In a culture that knows few Bible verses, this one has remained well-known. Many people outside the church consider Christians overly judgmental, so they quote this verse back to us with a certain "Gotcha!" vibe. I wish I could say they were wrong about our critical spirit. Too often, we deserve it.

After making this pithy statement, Jesus went on to tell a very funny story. Honestly, it reads like a comedy sketch. Get your improv group together, and give it a go. "Why do you look at the speck of sawdust in your brother's eye and pay no attention to the plank in your own eye?" (Matthew 7:3). Here, let me help you with that speck of dust. Don't worry about the huge log protruding from my eye. I can see just fine.

This is the blind spot I mentioned earlier. Consumed by a critical, judgmental spirit, people don't see what they don't see. They think they're qualified to do eye surgery on you when they themselves have seriously obstructed vision.

I like the way The Message expresses a parallel passage from Jesus:
Don't pick on people, jump on their failures, criticize their faults—unless, of course, you want the same treatment. Don't condemn those who are down; that hardness can boomerang. Be easy on people; you'll find life a lot easier. —Luke 6:37-38

FLATTERY

Let's go to the other extreme, the flattering side of this grid. Just as a critical spirit jettisons kindness and weaponizes candor, a flattering spirit does the same thing on the opposite side. In their effort to be kind (or appear that way), flatterers are willing to trash truth.

Critical — No Kindness, No Grace

Candid

Kind

Flattering — No Candor, No Truth

Many of us find this approach very tempting. We want to be nice to people, and we want them to like us. One great way to attract people is to say nice things about them—whether or not these things are true. Flattery will get you everywhere.

Without the bedrock of truth, flattery is flimsy. It's shallow. A house built on sand. Relationships cannot grow in this soil.

It's common for romances to start with flattery. The couple shares things they like about each other. Their mutual attraction is celebrated. But I maintain that their love won't really grow until they learn to be candid.

"I love you, but it annoys me when you do this."

"If this relationship is going to go anywhere, I need you to do this."

This isn't first-date banter, but as a couple considers spending their lives together, they will have to enter some deeply honest negotiations about a variety of needs, desires, and preferences. If they keep wading in the shallows of flattery, they'll never swim in the ocean of true love.

While the Bible promotes kindness, committed friendship, and love, it's no fan of flattery:

> Everyone lies to their neighbor; they flatter with their lips but harbor deception in their hearts. May the Lord silence all flattering lips. —Psalm 12:2-3

CANDID AND KIND

The early church had a problem with false teachers who left God's truth behind as they delivered an easier version of the gospel. In one passage, the apostle Paul predicted an onslaught of such flatterers in the end times: "To suit their own desires, [people] will gather around them a great number of teachers to say what their itching ears want to hear" (2 Timothy 4:3).

Ultimately, flattery is about scratching itches—and avoiding the full truth.

THE VALUE OF SUPPORTIVE CORRECTION

A friend of mine used to direct high school musicals. He was brought in as a freelancer to do the stage direction, working with a female teacher from the school who served as music director. This woman was demanding with high standards and an often critical manner. My friend's personality was completely different—gentle, supportive, and kind. He appreciated the music teacher's expertise, but he knew these kids were amateurs and didn't want to push them too hard.

In one rehearsal, a young actress worked with both these directors, repeating a scene she struggled with. After they finished and the music teacher had gone, the girl said to my friend, "I like your directing. You make me feel better."

He thought a moment and replied, "I may make you feel better, but she makes you better."

It was an important insight, and I've talked further with my friend about it. I suspect that both of these directors were operating on the Candid-Kind continuum—though they may have slid into the extremes. The music teacher had a candid style in her effort to hone the performances of her students, but she occasionally turned overly critical. Meanwhile, my friend showed kindness, though this might have slid into flattery.

His comment to the student is worth considering. He recognized that the music teacher's candid (and sometimes harsh) feedback was making the student a "better" performer. But I'd like to add a qualification. I think both of these directors, working in tandem, made the student a better performer. The teacher's candor showed the girl how to improve, but my friend's kindness kept her in the game.

It is the combination of truth and grace, being both candid and kind, that truly makes us good friends, parents, spouses, better leaders, and faithful and fruitful followers of Jesus.

> *It is the combination of truth and grace, being both candid and kind, that truly makes us good friends, parents, spouses, better leaders, and faithful and fruitful followers of Jesus.*

I know some critics think they're upholding truth, but they're actually missing a key element of the truth—the value of the person they're criticizing. When they tear someone down, they're saying, "You are a nothing. You will never amount to anything." That's simply false.

I know some flatterers think they're expressing a high degree of kindness, but they are wading in the shallow end of the pool. True kindness—God's kind of love—rejoices in the truth and expresses that truth as needed.

"Whoever rebukes a person will in the end gain favor rather than one who has a flattering tongue," says Proverbs 28:23.

"Wounds from a friend can be trusted, but an enemy multiplies kisses" (Proverbs 27:6).

In these and other passages, Scripture tells us that truth—honest, candid correction does not just balance out kindness. It is an expression of godly kindness. It's not a matter of being kind on Tuesday and candid on Wednesday. We show truth in our grace and grace in our truth!

We might find a modern proverb on this subject in Ted Lasso, one of my favorite TV series: "Remember, Ted, the truth will set you free. But it will piss you off first."

PARENTING

I think we see this clearly in the act of parenting. In chapter 8, I'll delve into this more fully, but here I just want to point out the importance of being both candid and kind together. The Bible tells us, "Direct your children onto the right path, and when they are older, they will not leave it" (Proverbs 25:6, NLT). We need to teach our kids the truth about God, themselves, and the world.

One of the most revered passages in the Hebrew Scriptures says this:

These commandments that I give you today are to be on your hearts. Impress them on your children. Talk about them when you sit at home and when you walk along the road, when you lie down and when you get up. Tie them as symbols on your hands and bind them on your foreheads. Write them on the doorframes of your houses and on your gates. —Deuteronomy 6:6-9

We've all seen examples of religious instruction gone wrong where overly critical parents alienate their children. Their efforts to indoctrinate them in biblical truth end up turning them away or even burning potential conversational bridges for the future.

The Bible also cautions parents, "Do not embitter your children, or they will become discouraged" (Colossians 3:21). We're given the example of God Himself: "The Lord is like a father to his children, tender and compassionate to those who fear him. For he knows how weak we are; he remembers we are only dust" (Psalm 103:13-14, NLT).

Parenting isn't easy. I know this firsthand. And I have sometimes vacillated between criticism and flattery, telling my children everything they need to know in order to function as adults someday or excusing everything they do because they're "just kids." The healthy tension I have tried to learn, even as I offer it to you, combines grace and truth—showing them the truth of God's Word as the moral compass for their lives and extending to them the same grace Jesus extends to me every day.

THE POWER OF KINDNESS

Let's talk more about kindness. One proverb has always puzzled me:
If your enemy is hungry, give him food to eat; if he is thirsty, give him water to drink. In doing this, you will heap burning coals on his head, and the Lord will reward you. —Proverbs 25:21-22 (quoted also in Romans 12:20)

This passage reminds me of a senior saint who is now with Jesus. Charlotte was a faithful supporter of my ministry and a sweet friend. When she passed away, her longtime friends relayed a special story about her childhood. She was bullied in elementary school. At recess, when no teacher was watching, a boy would push her into the dirt. Day after day, this happened.

When her mother learned about it, a plan was concocted. They bought a candy bar on the way to school. "When he comes up to you, just give him this candy bar," her mom said.

That's it. That was the only instruction she gave little Charlotte.

So that's what Charlotte did. At recess that day, before the boy could push her down, Charlotte quickly stretched out her hand to him, holding the candy bar. She didn't say a word. He snatched it out of her hand and walked off . . . without pushing her down.

Day two was Part two of Mom's plan: Do it again!

The next day Charlotte held out another candy bar.

The boy looked at her and asked, "Are you sure?"

She nodded.

The boy received it, said, "Thank you, Charlotte," and never bothered her again.

I'm still not sure about the coals of fire, but I know kindness packs a powerful punch.

I'm still not sure about the coals of fire, but I know kindness packs a powerful punch. Can we be creatively kind, even as we recognize the true value of the people we interact with?

CHAPTER 6

RUNNING AND RESTING

Sometimes, a Bible story gives us lots of detail, but it's still hard to figure out. That's the case in John 11 where Jesus was told of the fatal sickness of His friend Lazarus.

Instead of rushing to His buddy's bedside and healing him, Jesus stayed put. For two days, He remained where He was, encamped on the east side of the Jordan River, where He was likely preaching about the kingdom of heaven and healing the sick as He did throughout His earthly ministry.

Why did He wait? Why didn't He immediately rush to the aid of His close friend?

Well, for one thing, it was dangerous. The hometown of Lazarus and his sisters was just around the bend from Jerusalem where the religious leaders had threatened to kill Jesus. The disciples assumed that Jesus wanted to stay on the safe side of the Jordan, and they were good with that. Yet Jesus did make this trip two days later, suggesting that safety wasn't His primary concern.

We can better understand the story when we see that Jesus's waiting was a matter of timing.

When Jesus finally arrived at His friend's tomb, Lazarus had been dead for four days. The grieving sisters seemed to scold Jesus for dawdling. If He had been there earlier, they said, He could have healed their brother. Jesus proceeded to do something even more shocking—in front of a crowd. He stood at the tomb of the dead man and shouted for him to come out.

Suspicious onlookers may have accused Him of having no respect for the dead. People were probably worried about the smell of a body buried in a tomb for four days. In the midst of their wondering, heads began to turn, jaws began to drop, and eyes homed in on a man wrapped in burial clothes, hopping out of a grave like a man trying to take his pants off without removing his shoes first. There he was! Lazarus had come back to life.

Scholars tell us that, according to ancient Jewish tradition, it takes as long as three days for the spirit to leave a dead body. Maybe that contributed to Jesus's sense of timing. Perhaps He wanted to ensure that Lazarus was unquestionably dead before He worked this astonishing miracle. This wasn't just CPR, reviving a swooning patient. The body was wrapped up, lying in a tomb, and decaying when Jesus provided new life.

This chapter is about timing—specifically, what you do with your time. Sometimes we rush somewhere to do something important, and sometimes we stay put; we rest.

Jesus is a great example of both those things—running and resting. At one point, His family feared He was running Himself ragged. They wanted to stage an intervention, to take Him home and give Him a break (see Luke 3:20-21). Yet we also know that Jesus refueled by spending time alone with His heavenly Father (see Luke 5:15-16). His ministry wasn't just run-run-run; He rested too. And through it all, He seemed to follow a divine timetable.

> *Throughout Jesus's ministry, He seemed to follow a divine timetable.*

RUNNING

"*Is your refrigerator running?*"
"*I need to run to the store.*"
"*I've got a runny nose.*"
"*The shop is running a sale.*"
"*They keep running their mouth.*"

"Running" means activity. We humans are meant to be active as well: "The Lord God took the man and put him in the Garden of Eden to work it and take care of it" (Genesis 2:15, emphasis added). Sometimes, we imagine this original "paradise" as merely a vacation spot, with the first couple lounging all day beside the Euphrates, sipping mango juice. Not so. While the garden was full of "trees that were pleasing to the eye and good for food" (verse 9), Adam and Eve still had a job to do. We can assume it wasn't drudgery; it was productive.

Our bodies need activity. Muscles atrophy when we don't use them. Food turns to fat. Healthy living requires regular exercise. So if you haven't budged from your couch all week, streaming nine seasons of your favorite sitcom back-to-back, something's wrong. Go for a walk. Play some pickleball. Wash your car.

But I'm not just talking about physical activity. There's a spiritual aspect to our human activity as well. Hebrews 12:1 says, "Let us run with perseverance the race marked out for us." Several other Bible passages refer to our lives as a race we run, urging us to run it well (see 1 Corinthians 9:24 and Galatians 2:2).

God calls us to do things—to use the abilities He has given us for good purposes. I love how obvious the apostle Paul gets when talking about spiritual gifts. I mentioned this in chapter 4: "If your gift is prophesying, then prophesy . . . if it is serving, then serve; if it is teaching, then teach," and so on (Romans 12:6-7). Don't just say, "Look at me! I'm gifted!" Use your gift to get stuff done.

Some of us are fortunate to work full-time in jobs that use our God-given gifts and talents. But there are many whose daily work is "just a job." They earn a living, but they doubt their work contributes much to the good of humanity.

When I encounter people in this situation, I assure them they can still "run the race." They can develop redemptive relationships at work and dedicate the quality of their work to the Lord. After all, Paul wrote to slaves, "Whatever you do, work at it with all your heart, as working for the Lord, not for human masters" in Colossians 3:23.

Develop redemptive relationships at work and dedicate the quality of your work to the Lord.

I urge them to find other areas in which to serve—perhaps at church or for a community charity—some way to use their giftedness to help others and glorify God. And don't neglect opportunities for learning, Christian fellowship, or prayer. Spiritual growth can happen quietly by yourself, but often, it occurs in group activities as believers encourage one another.

Is your spiritual life running?

RESTING

After centuries of making bricks in Egypt, the Israelites probably had no clue what a "day off" was. However, at Mount Sinai, God wrote it into their contract: "Six days you shall labor and do all your work, but the seventh day is a sabbath to the Lord your God. On it you shall not do any work" (Exodus 20:9-10). This was their new schedule, based on a principle as old as creation. "For in six days the Lord made the heavens and the earth, the sea, and all that is in them, but he rested on the seventh day" (verse 11).

People needed rest. Animals needed rest. Even the land needed rest. (And the Law required farmland to lie fallow every seventh year.)

After all our talk about the importance of human activity, we now come to the flip side of this healthy tension. Along with our running, we also need "Resting."

Most obviously, we need periods of physical rest after strenuous activity. If your daily work involves a lot of movement, you probably have breaks built into your schedule, allowing your body to relax a while before resuming work. I talked with a teacher who had just returned to her job after six weeks at home, recovering from surgery. She was surprised at how worn out she felt after her first day back. "I wasn't doing anything—just standing," she said. But a full day of standing after a month of rest takes its toll. In a similar way, parents of young children may underestimate their need for physical rest after extended times of scooping up, holding, or chasing their kids. That's why we don't consider trips with our kids "vacations." We call them "adventures" because, many times, Janet and I need a vacation from our vacation. Just ask anyone who has taken their child to Disney World.

We also need mental rest after our minds are running all day. This is true for executives and admins alike and drivers, artists, and preachers. We might sit at a desk for hours, but our brains are whirring away, wearying us. We need rest in order to clear our heads—listening to music, playing a video game, or any kind of "mindless" activity.

Some people need social rest. This is especially true of introverts who expend energy when they're with others but regain energy when alone. I know one guy, very active in his church, who might have three or four church-related meetings during the week. After weeks like that, he sometimes stays home on Sunday, watching the service online. "I'm all peopled out," he says apologetically. I believe in the importance of corporate worship, but I get it. He needs private time to refuel.

In our modern age, we also need technological rest. I've become aware that Zoom meetings carry a special kind of stress. While it makes meetings more convenient for many, the slight lag and tech issues can make communication a bit more difficult. Without realizing it, we miss out on body language and some facial cues that occur in physical interactions. Our eyes become fatigued after hours of interacting solely through a screen. So if you feel wiped out after a day of online meetings, there are reasons for that. You need rest. The same might be said for teenagers who spend a vast amount of time each day on their phones. Take a break!

I believe there's also a need for spiritual rest. Especially in the evangelical-Pentecostal tradition, great emphasis is placed on Christian activity: prayer, Bible study, fellowship, witnessing, charitable functions, volunteering to serve, etc. We leaders often put pressure on people—explicitly or implicitly—to do lots of things in order to prove themselves as good Christians. Some people burn out. Some lose the joy of their faith. Resting spiritually means allowing God to restore and renew our spirits. It's taking time to listen to the Holy Spirit, letting Him bring us back into proper alignment with Jesus. Spiritual rest is recalibration that ensures we stay focused on God's plans and purposes for our lives. We all need moments to push the reset button in every area.

The Lord says, "Be still, and know that I am God" (Psalm 46:10). There is great value in slowing down, focusing not on all the things you do for God but resting in what He has done for us.

THE COMBINATION

Did you know that shoes need rest? It's true of different materials used to make different kinds of footwear. The foam in running shoes needs nearly two days to recover from the pounding of your morning jog. Leather also needs recovery time, I understand. So it's best not to wear the same shoes every day. If you buy two pairs and alternate between them, experts say, they'll last much longer.

But it's not good to leave the shoes in your closet for lengthy periods, either. Shoes need to be worn. The materials get "broken in," becoming more supple, molded to your feet.

Like us, shoes need a rhythm of running and resting.

Our bodies are designed to go to bed tired. It's hard to get a good night's rest if you've loafed around all day. And most of us know how a lack of rest impairs our activities the next day. The pattern feeds itself: run hard, rest well, run some more, rest some more. At our local shoe store, you can go and stand on a machine, and it will read all that is wrong with your step, your arch, your foot, where you carry your weight, etc. Sometimes, we need this in our daily life—an appraisal of where we are leaning, where we need more rest, where we are placing our weight, where we need more support, etc.

I'll confess it. I'm not very good at taking vacations. Never have been. I'm an active guy. It's hard to shut things down for a week or two. I recently read an article that said people become so worked up as they go on vacation (between budgeting, packing, airlines, car rental, figuring out the hotel, planning the sight-seeing, etc.) that most people need three days to recover, and then they can begin to enjoy their vacation physically and mentally. In other words, the first three days of your vacay, you're still amped up. We can't even begin to really relax until day four.

Apparently, resting can be hard work.

Recently, I was sort of forced into an unexpected resting situation, and it worked out very well. My wife and I were planning to join her parents in celebrating their fiftieth wedding anniversary on a Hawaii getaway. We had all sorts of activities planned for them and for us. But at the last minute, during a connecting flight, a surprising and scary health issue arose that kept my in-laws from going.

As we made an emergency landing, we had to figure out what to do. Janet and I were of a mind to just cancel the trip entirely, but my in-laws, being their selfless selves, said, "Go! Enjoy! There's nothing you can do for us here." So my wife and I celebrated her parents' anniversary in fine fashion—but without them.

That was weird—but good. It gave us some much-needed time together, but it also gave us a stretch of time with a lot less planned. We had canceled most of the celebratory activities we had planned for my in-laws. It just didn't feel right to do those without them. So we had a week on this island paradise with nothing to do but rest.

That sounds exquisite to you, doesn't it? But for a "what's the plan," go-get-'em guy like me, it was a challenge. Still, we quickly adapted. Our place had a deck with a grill, so we spent the early evening cooking our dinner—an activity we could do together and something different from our normal pattern at home. In between these simple activities, we just lounged. We could get only one channel on the TV in our room, and for some reason, it only played the Deal or No Deal game show—all day, every day.

We became experts on Howie Mandel.

That's a sentence I never thought I'd write—or even think.

I suppose if we ever face a situation where we have to select a suitcase which may or may not have a lot of cash, we'll know exactly what to look for. But it's hard to imagine any specific value to all this TV-watching. We were just chilling out.

Was that a waste? Should we feel guilty for squandering these God-given hours on something so trivial? No! We needed the downtime. God has designed all of us for running and resting. He has given us work to do, but He reminds us clearly in Scripture that rest should also be part of our schedule. I learned that I need to know when to rest. I need to recognize when to run. And through it all, how to go with a little more flow and have fun when things don't go as planned. It may just be the best thing for your plan.

> *God has given us work to do, but He reminds us clearly in Scripture that rest should also be part of our schedule.*

THE COMPLACENT LIFE

The NBA tries not to give teams back-to-back games. Sometimes, it's unavoidable, but in general, if you play Monday, you'll get to rest on Tuesday. Running and jumping for forty-eight minutes plus slamming your body against defenders who don't want you to run and jump, well, that takes a lot out of you. Your body needs the rest in order to come back strong on Wednesday.

On the occasions when teams must play back-to-back, the results aren't pretty. Fans can see their favorite players dragging, shots falling short. On average, teams lose 56 percent of their games when they've played the day before. Athletes need rest. Their bodies need restoration.

As with the other healthy tensions in this book, we see the two good things—Running and Resting—interconnecting in the center of a grid, with two dangerous developments on the outside.

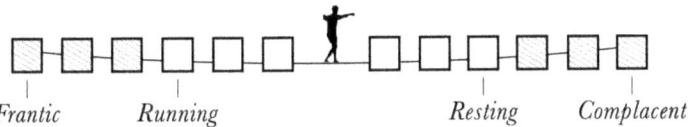

Frantic   *Running*   *Resting*   *Complacent*

Again we see our subtraction principle at work. Subtract resting from running, and you get a "Frantic" attitude, nonstop activity, and continual urgency. It's like we're always on the back end of back-to-back games.

On the other side of the grid, if we take away running from resting, we're "Complacent"—with no desire for any activity. In essence, we're removing the restorative purpose of resting. We aren't resting up in order to get back in the game. A complacent person has dropped out of the game entirely.

It wasn't so long ago that a worldwide pandemic forced many of us into a period of relative inactivity. Schools, stores, and restaurants were closed. Some churches, too. Business meetings were held online. Of course, the regulations were different from place to place, and I recognize that healthcare workers, delivery drivers, educators, and parents of young children were forced into frantic activity during this time. But many others experienced a slowdown. Movie-going was radically down while movie-streaming was at an all-time high.

I think some people have stayed "shut down," even after the worst of the pandemic. While the rest of society gets back to a kind of normalcy, some prefer staying home, streaming TV shows, getting food delivered, and so on. I see something similar in people who retire after many years of work. They withdraw from activities and relationships, dropping out, shutting down.

What's wrong with that? If you want to slow down the pace of your life, that's fine. But I see unhealthy consequences when people stop connecting, contributing, or caring.

"Am I my brother's keeper?" the first murderer asked (see Genesis 4). Apparently, his answer was no, but ours is yes. Jesus made it clear that we are connected to others. We read that "Love your neighbor as yourself" (see Matthew 22:49) was one of Jesus's answers to the Pharisees in chapter 2 when they asked Him what the most important commandments were. Slow your pace if you want, but we all bear a responsibility to love one another. The New Testament urges, "Let us consider how we may spur one another on toward love and good deeds, not giving up meeting together, as some are in the habit of doing, but encouraging one another" (Hebrews 10:24-25).

When I talk about "contributing," I don't mean money. I'm talking about the unique abilities, experiences, and ideas you have to share with those around you. When you pull yourself out of the game, you're depriving teammates of your valuable contributions.

One of the saddest things is when people stop caring. There is a kind of atrophy that happens to our heart and soul when we let a much-needed rest turn into a dangerous complacency. Perhaps you are in a transitional time, changing the things you care most about, but don't stop caring entirely.

Perhaps you are in a transitional time, changing the things you care most about, but don't stop caring entirely.

The book of Proverbs offers caution for young people in danger of developing a complacent attitude.

> *I walked by the field of a lazy person, the vineyard of one with no common sense. I saw that it was overgrown with nettles. It was covered with weeds, and its walls were broken down. Then, as I looked and thought about it, I learned this lesson: A little extra sleep, a little more slumber, a little folding of the hands to rest—then poverty will pounce on you like a bandit; scarcity will attack you like an armed robber.*
> —Proverbs 24:30-34 (NLT)

To the young recipients of this age-old teaching, the warning had to do with poverty. But for adults who are letting go of important parts of their life, it's a warning against "scarcity"—perhaps a scarcity of love or joy.

Get back in the game. Don't let a creeping complacency rob you of the best things in life.

THE FRANTIC EXTREME

About fifty years ago, a Baptist seminary professor coined the term *workaholic*. People instantly understood the concept. They knew what an alcoholic was, and they knew people who were driven to work in the same way others were driven to drink. In the decades since, psychologists have refined the concept. Is there a chemical aspect to this problem? Do workaholics get a "high" when they work? At what point does it become dangerous?

It's a fascinating field of study, but I'm not going to answer those questions here. I will say that work without rest is not the way God designed us. We might enjoy our work. We might find excitement in our work that we find nowhere else. We might be overwhelmed by the amount of work to do, so we can't even think about stopping. As Christians, we might feel compelled to work for the Lord nonstop—worshiping, evangelizing, and feeding the hungry. How can we ease up when Jesus sacrificed His all for us?

But if we never take time to recover, restore, or refuel, we're ignoring a rhythm of life that God has established.

> *If we never take time to recover, restore, or refuel, we're ignoring a rhythm of life that God has established.*

A workaholic operates at a frantic pace. Busy-ness is the boss, and there's always something more to do. Who has time to rest? While some workaholics say they enjoy life that way, it's not healthy in any sustainable way. They may pride themselves on great productivity, but this may be an illusion.

Some time ago, a Christian writer wrote a booklet called Tyranny of the Urgent, and the idea proved extremely helpful to business planners ever since. The point is that many businesses (including churches and charities) are so focused on putting out fires (the urgent) that they never plan wisely for the future. It applies to personal planning as well. The person who runs from one activity to the next, responding to the needs of the moment, takes no time for the long view. What kind of life do they really want? How can they be most productive? How can they succeed in all areas of their life in a balanced way? When "the urgent" plays tyrant, people soon neglect their health, their families, and their faith.

We find a description of this in the book of Ecclesiastes. I love The Message rendering here, catching the root image of the Hebrew word for "vanity" or "emptiness" as a wisp of smoke:

> *I turned my head and saw yet another wisp of smoke on its way to nothingness: a solitary person, completely alone—no children, no family, no friends—yet working obsessively late into the night, compulsively greedy for more and more, never bothering to ask, "Why am I working like a dog, never having any fun? And who cares?" More smoke. A bad business.*
> —Ecclesiastes 4:7-8

For me, the fear of complacency can drive me to the frantic extreme. I feel so driven—overwhelmed by the need to achieve, perform, and do great things for God. I don't want anyone to think I am complacent, so I run the red line to ensure that is never the case. The truth is, God didn't design me—or you—for either of these extremes.

NETWORKING

The frantic life doesn't just appear in the business world. Increasingly, we see it in social media networks. These platforms—Facebook, Twitter, TikTok, and a host of others—are cleverly (and even creepily) designed to scratch your informational itches. They learn what you like, and they give you more of it. Algorithms aren't just for college calculus anymore. They script our screen content and manipulate our focus. And it's working, big time.

Americans spend an average of 2.5 hours each day on social media, and that number has been going up steadily. For the youngest Americans, that number has been exploding. Tweens (ages 8-12) reportedly spend 5.5 hours a day on social media. For teenagers (13-17), it's 8.5 hours.

Stop. Think about that. Teenagers spend half their waking life in the world of social media.

Many things could be said about the content of social media, but I won't say them here. Right now, my only point is that these platforms are designed to create urgency. You like that post? Here's another, even better. Don't you want to see how these celebrities react? Watch what this cat does next. You'll never believe what's behind this... click to find out. How many friends do you have? How many followers?

The algorithm is an All-Go rhythm.

(See what I did there? Now tweet that out to all your friends and post it on Facebook with a picture of your Bible and coffee cup.)

Go-go-go-go-go. You have to see what's next. Don't miss what your friends are saying about what the athlete said about what the actress said about the royal couple. You don't want to miss out on what's happening!

Technology has made our lives—and the lives of our younger generations—frantic.

THE CONTROL CIRCLE

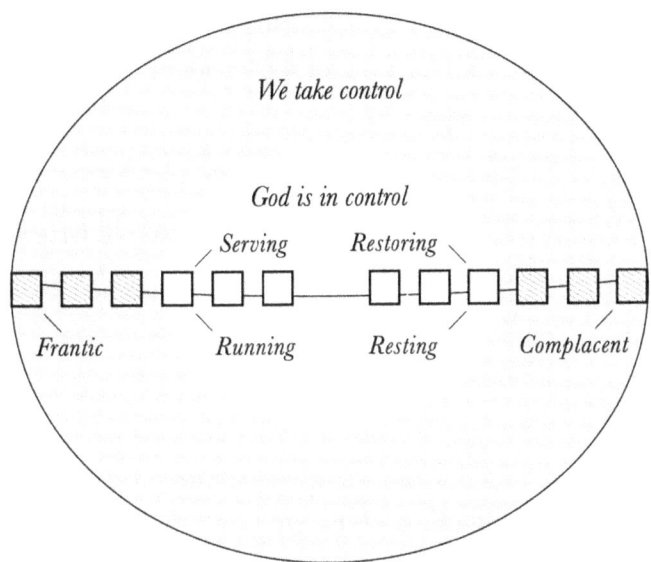

As you can see, the healthy tension of the center circle allows us to run and rest, to take time to serve and to be restored. We are able to do this when God is in control at the center of our lives. When we become frantic or complacent, we are taking control, grabbing the steering wheel, and demanding our own way.

In talking about confidence and humility, we saw that the extremes shared a common trait. Whether you're arrogant or ashamed, you're focusing on yourself. Now we see the same pattern with the extremes of running and resting. Within that healthy tension, we observe a pattern of service and patience. We work, and sometimes we settle back and let God do His restorative work in us. But in the extremes of being frantic or complacent, we tend to shut God out of the picture. We feel our own compulsion to accomplish as much as possible, or we reject all productive effort. Even when we think we're frantically serving God, we're not following God's rhythm of work and rest. And often, those manic efforts to do great things for God end up backfiring—exalting only ourselves or dragging down the true work of the kingdom.

We work, and sometimes we settle back and let God do His restorative work in us.

On those occasions, we look a lot like King Saul. Acting when he should have waited and waiting when he should have acted, Saul always seemed out of step with God's desires. I believe an important part of the Resting/Restoring process is to recalibrate our connection with God, to get in tune and in step with Him again.

Let's let Jesus be our model. As we read about Jesus's earthly ministry, we see that He worked hard. He ministered tirelessly, healing the sick, caring for those in need, and sharing God's love with the unloved. We also see rhythms of rest in Jesus's earthly life. He spent consistent time alone with His heavenly Father, away from the demands and questions of the crowd and His students. We see Jesus taking naps (though sometimes interrupted by frantic storm-fearing disciples). During intense seasons of ministry, we see Him getting away from the crowds to rest and urging His disciples to do the same.

As Jesus said in response to legalistic comments from skeptical religious leaders: "The Sabbath was made for man, not man for the Sabbath" (Mark 2:27, ESV). That day of rest is God's gift to His image-bearers. Our Lord enables us to practice rhythms of work and rest. Neither is as effective as God intended without the other. When running and resting ebb and flow in a healthy tension in our lives, we experience the abundant life Jesus modeled for us and died to get us.

"Be still before the Lord and wait patiently for him," says the psalmist. "Do not fret when people succeed in their ways, when they carry out their wicked schemes" (Psalm 37:7). Often, we want to jump into the fray, fighting against those "wicked schemes," but Scripture often calls us back to the Lord's rhythms. When we "wait" for the Lord, great things happen.

My dad and I set a "let's do this together" goal a few years back. It was my thirty-fifth birthday year and his fifty-fifth. We decided that for our 35/55 we would run a marathon together. Our big challenge was finding a way to train together while living states apart (my dad in Kansas, I in Texas). Nevertheless, we went for it. We logged our times and compared them, keeping our cadences close together. We navigated weather, crazy schedules, and injuries here and there. But we put in the work.

The day of the race finally came. We met each other in California for the Orange County marathon. Six miles in, Dad experienced a severe cramp in his calf. He had to lie down in the grass at the side of the road. He told me to just finish without him. Frankly, we both were quite overemotional in the moment. We had come too far to quit now, and there was no way I was going to run by myself—because I wasn't really there for the race. I was there to be with my dad. I wasn't going on without him. I began rubbing his calf (he would appreciate my saying here that his calf muscles are like a bodybuilder's), and after a few minutes, the cramp went away. We got back on track, and we finished the race.

> *As you run through life together with Him, He will massage the sore spots.*

In that moment, I waited on him, and later, Dad would wait on me. But as encouraging as those moments were, there is nothing like the God of the cosmos. As you wait on Him, as you spend time with Him, as you run through life together with Him, He will massage the sore spots. He will never leave or forsake. He's not going to have you run alone.

"But those who wait on the Lord shall renew their strength; They shall mount up with wings like eagles, They shall run and not be weary, They shall walk and not faint" (Isaiah 40:31, NKJV).

CHAPTER 7

LISTENING AND SPEAKING

Mom and Dad thought the boy was with friends elsewhere in the caravan. He was twelve years old, quite able to frolic with playmates, not needing to check in all the time. Besides, He was a good kid, not likely to get into trouble.

The whole family had enjoyed the festival in the big city, and now they were on their four-day journey home. But in the evening, when all the young 'uns found their families again, young Jesus was nowhere to be found. Worried sick, Mary and Joseph bolted back to Jerusalem and searched for the boy. Finally, they spotted Him in the temple complex, meeting with a group of rabbis, "listening to them and asking them questions" (Luke 2:46).

We interrupt this family drama to zero in on what young Jesus was doing—and how we might follow His example. The biblical text says, "Everyone who heard him was amazed at his understanding and his answers" (Luke 2:47).

With the benefit of history, we look back on this account and say, "Of course, this boy would school the scholars! He was the Son of God!" We know who He grew up to be. We can imagine the surprise of the teachers at the wisdom of this precocious child, and we deeply sympathize with the parents who were still figuring out how to raise the Messiah.

But Jesus wasn't just sharing the secrets of eternity; He was "listening . . . and asking questions." This was a two-way conversation. They were amazed at His answers, but He prodded them for answers too. We don't know the content of this conversation, but we get some ideas from the many questions Jesus asked throughout His adult life.

> Who is the "neighbor" we're supposed to love?
> What kind of "rest" does God really want on the Sabbath Day?
> "Who do you say that I am?"
> "Where are your accusers?"
> How do you read the law?
> If the Messiah is David's "son," why does he call him "Lord" in the Psalms?

As an adult, Jesus called people into a new understanding of God, of reality, of faith. He challenged the accepted and assumed ideas of His culture. Routinely, He did this by asking questions, stirring thoughts, and sometimes, stimulating discussions. So it's not really a surprise to see Him doing the same things at age twelve. (I realize, however, that this creates some challenging expectations for modern preteens. I can't get my twelve-year-old to stop dancing "the Griddy," and there's young Jesus presenting a master class to the spiritual leaders of His day. No pressure, kid.)

Jesus had plenty to say, of course, and the teachers were "amazed" at what they heard, but this wasn't just a show put on by a child prodigy. Jesus drew them into a conversation. In this, He gave us a model to follow in our own interactions. Again, you've got to get this! If Jesus, God of the cosmos in human form, who knows everything, took the time to ask good questions and listen to what people had to say, how much more do we need to do the same?

> *Speech is not just for transmitting information. It's for building relationships.*

Speech is not just for transmitting information. It's for building relationships. And, as with everything else we're called to do as His followers, it's for showing love.

HEARD INSTINCT

My friend James was telling about a lunch he had with a woman he knew, a long-time colleague. Over the years, they had often shared ideas about their work, but this time the colleague talked about various problems in her personal life. James wanted to help, and he thought of various things he could say to try to fix her problems.

"But then I realized I didn't have the answers," James told me. "I couldn't fix her situation. The best thing I could do was to ask her questions. Maybe, as she clarified things in our conversation, she might get some ideas of how to improve matters. But this didn't really happen either, and afterward, I felt kind of bad that I hadn't said the right thing to help her."

But the next day, he got a text from her thanking him. "It was nice to be heard," she wrote. Maybe, in that conversation, it was all he needed to do.

I suspect that's true of most conversations. The friends of Job had the right idea when they sat down with him for a week, sharing his woes in silence. That's right. The Bible tells us that "they sat on the ground with him seven days and nights, but no one spoke a word to him because they saw his suffering was very intense" (Job 2:13, CSB). They actually got into trouble when they started talking, trying to explain his problems, trying to fix him.

Our next healthy tension is between "Speaking" and "Listening." Scripture says there is "a time to be silent and a time to speak" (Ecclesiastes 3:7). So, yes, there is a time to voice your love, your prayers, your concerns—but as I look at the world around us, I beg you to lean way into listening. It's easy to assume that our words are helpful and necessary when they aren't.

"Everyone should be quick to listen, slow to speak and slow to become angry," says the biblical James (1:19). From his epistle, we can figure out that he was speaking to religious people who were having a lot of arguments. Why else would he warn about the destructive power of the tongue? He called them out for quarreling and slander. "Those who consider themselves religious and yet do not keep a tight rein on their tongues deceive themselves, and their religion is worthless" (James 1:26; see also 3:3-8; 4:1-2, 11).

Hmmm. Do you have any friends on social media who need to read James? Are you the social media "friend" who needs to read

James? In today's world, we might all need a refresher course on that New Testament epistle. We need to understand that a "tight rein on our tongues" includes a tight rein on our thumbs.

> *We need to understand that a "tight rein on our tongues" includes a tight rein on our thumbs.*

In the Old Testament, the book of Proverbs has similar advice. *The one who has knowledge uses words with restraint, and whoever has understanding is even-tempered. Even fools are thought wise if they keep silent, and discerning if they hold their tongues.* —Proverbs 17:27-28

This is just an older version of "slow to speak, slow to become angry." And I love the fact that "even fools" can seem wise . . . until they start talking. This is evidenced every day on every news channel and social media platform—and around every Thanksgiving table with Uncle Larry.

ACTIVE LISTENING

The healthy tension between speaking and listening does not mean that you mute yourself and check out of the conversation. Listening doesn't just happen in the ears. It involves the whole brain and usually a set of natural physical responses. And it often includes some speaking as well.

(By the way, this is why online video calls can be so stressful. The brief lag throws off the natural rhythm of facial and vocal cues that indicate people are paying attention, so speakers don't get the emotional reinforcement they're used to. This doesn't mean we throw away a tool for communication and connection that is useful in its own right. It does mean that we all need to work extra hard to listen online.)

A generation ago, marriage counselors began talking about "active listening." It's a valuable concept. Wives and husbands, they said, carry on conversations with different styles and different assumptions—as if they're speaking different languages. One way to deal with this is "active listening"—clarifying, repeating, and asking questions.

It turns out this technique isn't just for marriages. It makes anyone a better conversation partner, interacting moment by moment with what the other person is saying.

Questions are key.

By asking questions, I ensure that I understand the full intent of what I'm hearing. I can ask about emotional context: How did you feel when that happened? Through questions, I give permission to the person to keep talking, knowing that I'm interested in what they have to say.

As I read the Gospels, I'm amazed at how many questions Jesus asked. Now, certainly, He had a lot of good things to say, but He often chose to listen to others and used questions to learn what they were thinking and feeling.

Do you want to be healed?

Who do you say I am?

Do you love me?

He had a knack for getting to the heart of an issue—and to the heart of a person. As a proverb states, "The purposes of a person's heart are deep waters, but one who has insight draws them out" (Proverbs 20:5).

> *Jesus had a knack for getting to the heart of an issue—and to the heart of a person.*

We can follow His example by listening carefully and asking good questions. Questions that get to the heart of a matter. Questions that lead to greater clarity. That means more than just waiting your turn to speak or planning your next statement while the other person is talking and certainly not figuring out how to tear down their arguments. Listen for what they care about, for how they see the world, and ask questions to draw them out. Build better relationships by paying attention.

In the Bible's third chapter, God entered the Garden of Eden for His daily stroll, but Adam and Eve were hiding. The Lord asked a question. "Where are you?" (Genesis 3:9)

Now surely the omniscient Creator knew their GPS location. If questions were only about information, there would be no need to ask anything. He asked the question to draw them out, quite literally, to bring them out of hiding, to initiate an encounter with them after their fateful sin. And it worked.

But that's not the first question recorded in Scripture. Earlier in that same chapter, the serpent approached Eve and asked,

"Did God really say, 'You must not eat from any tree in the garden'?" (Genesis 3:1)

It was a challenge, twisting God's words and manipulating Eve. It set up the tempter's lies.

Even today, some questions are like that. These days, many questions are like that—manipulative, twisting, and deceiving. People invent "Gotcha!" questions to tear down their political foes. Reporters invent no-win queries—"Are you going to give back the money you stole?" Social media channels overflow with mic-drop moments when people think they've exposed the inconsistencies in opposing positions. Their questions aren't about clarifying anything, just muddying the waters. They're not designed to build relationships but to win a brutal game. The askers don't seem to be listening at all, just barking their opinion in the form of a question.

Do you see? What God creates, the enemy loves to counterfeit. God uses questions to bring us to truth, but the enemy likes to ask questions to stir up confusion and conflict. If the Savior of the world touched people's souls by asking insightful questions, how important is it for us to cultivate this art as well?

With my own family and friends, I've noticed how shallow questions yield shallow answers—and do nothing to build relationships. How many times have you asked someone, "How are you?" without really wanting to know? (Occasionally, we're surprised or even annoyed when people bend our ear for several minutes actually answering that question!)

When I ask my kids broad questions like, "How was your day?" I get shrugs and mumbles. But if I zero in on something they've told me previously—"How do you feel about that assignment you were working on?"—it shows that I'm listening and truly want to know about their feelings. It's more likely to open a conversation. The quality of my question determines the clarity of the answer.

The quality of the question determines the clarity of the answer.

When my kids were little, and they would hop in the car after school, I would ask crazy, random questions, questions that made them laugh but also think. For example, "If aliens invaded your school today, who would you want them to take back to their planet?" After throwing their head back with laughter, my kids would usually thrill me with a long, hilarious response. This is an example of how questions work at any age. Because at any age, people want to be heard.

As you've surely experienced many times, good conversations strike a healthy balance between speaking and listening. Questions provide a bridge between those two actions. You're speaking and moving the conversation forward, but you're preparing to listen.

EXTREMES

If you are constantly speaking and never listening, you are "Dominating." This is my term for one unhealthy extreme. Subtract listening from a good conversation, and that's what remains. Domination. What you have to say seems more important than the thoughts of others. Suddenly, you're singing a solo.

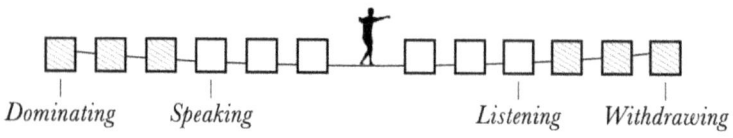

Dominating   *Speaking*   *Listening*   *Withdrawing*

I call the other unhealthy extreme "Withdrawing." Sometimes we sabotage conversations by tapping the mute button. We stop contributing. We might still be hearing, to some extent, but we've signed out.

This can happen for a number of rather valid reasons. Maybe we're intimidated by the speaker and unsure of the value of our own ideas. Maybe we can't get a word in edgewise, so we stop trying. Maybe we're just tired.

More than once, I've done this in meetings. Someone is presenting important info, and I'm listening, but I just don't have the energy to ask that clarifying question to make it a true conversation. And there have been times when I've been the speaker, and I saw the eyes of my audience glazing over. They're withdrawing; it's time for me to stop dominating.

It is crucial for married couples to embrace the healthy tension of speaking and listening—and avoid the extremes of dominating and withdrawing. People have different capacities for conversation, and spouses must learn this about themselves and each other. It might be perfectly fine for one spouse to talk two-thirds of the time if the other spouse is ready to listen that much. You may find your own rhythm, your own balance, but allow for your differences, and make some accommodations for the good of your relationship.

And, as I've said, questions help you calibrate this tension to a healthy level. Develop the art of asking questions that invite honest, creative responses and ultimately deepen your connections with others.

> *Develop the art of asking questions that invite honest, creative responses and ultimately deepen your connections with others.*

Think about that right now. Whom could you get to know a little better by simply asking a few of these questions below?

1) What do you miss about being a kid?
2) If someone gave you enough money to start a business—no strings attached—what kind of business would you want to start and why?
3) If you could go back in time, what's one piece of advice you'd give to your younger self?
4) What's something you want to do in the next year that you've never done before?
5) Tell me three things that happened in the last week that you're thankful for.
6) What's your favorite memory we've shared together? Gimme as many details as possible.
7) What makes you happy?
8) Who or what has changed your life?
9) How do you best connect with others?[1]

---

[1] Team Lemonade, "52 Questions for Deeper Conversations," *Lemonade Blog*, www.lemonade.com/blog/creating-meaningful-conversations/.

SHARING THE GOOD NEWS

For Christians, the tension between listening and speaking comes into play as we attempt to share our faith with others. Evangelical churches—with the Greek word for "good news" (*evangel*) embedded in that term—emphasize the importance of telling people about Jesus, but a lot of people have difficulty with this.

Some feel they don't know enough. Others aren't sure they have the skills to persuade people. But for many, it's a matter of politeness. It seems rude to urge your religious beliefs on someone else.

The Bible has three distinct sets of teaching on this matter, and we should learn from them all.

Speak it

Jesus clearly gave His disciples the commission to "go and make disciples" among people from all nations, teaching what He had taught them (Matthew 28:19). "Go into all the world and preach the Good News," He told them (Mark 16:15, NLT). He said they would be "witnesses," testifying about Him (Acts 1:8).

These are speaking words. Teach. Preach. Testify. "How shall they hear without a preacher?" Paul asked in Romans 10:14 (KJV), and in 2 Corinthians 5:18-20, he wrote about Christians carrying out the "ministry of reconciliation" with the clear message: "Be reconciled to God!"

Clearly, there is a crucial message to be shared verbally.

Yet for too long, we have allowed preachers to assume that the end justifies the means. As long as people raise their hand or walk the sawdust trail or pray the sinner's prayer, it doesn't matter what emotional abuse it takes to get them there. But that can't be true.

Scripture makes it clear that religious actions done without love are worthless, and this includes preaching: "If I speak God's Word with power, revealing all his mysteries and making everything plain as day . . . but I don't love, I'm nothing" (1 Corinthians 13:2, MSG).

As I see it, evangelists with incredibly rude attitudes who seek to manipulate and intimidate have left the healthy tension of speaking and listening, sliding into the danger zone of dominating. In contrast, the message of the gospel is most effective when spoken with grace and truth, as we see modeled by Jesus in His evangelistic preaching and teaching.

Live It

There's a controversial quote often credited to Francis of Assisi (though he probably didn't say it): "Preach the gospel at all times. When necessary, use words."

This bothers some people who think it gives Christians an excuse not to talk about their faith. But we don't need to see this through an either/or lens. The Bible gives us both angles: preaching the good news and living it out. "Let your light shine before others," Jesus said, "that they may see your good deeds and glorify your Father in heaven" (Matthew 5:16).

That "light" image is echoed elsewhere in Scripture. We are called to "shine . . . like stars in the sky," in a "warped and crooked generation" (Philippians 2:15).

We're also exhorted to "be wise in the way you act toward outsiders; make the most of every opportunity" (Colossians 4:5). Our either/or has turned into a both/and. We live a life of love and light before those who don't know Jesus, and we use words when necessary, making the most of opportunities to speak about Him.

LISTEN... AND ANSWER

We don't need to dominate conversations in order to get God's truth across. Instead, we observe a healthy tension of speaking and listening in our relationships. In these interactions, our Christ-centered attitudes are on display. We're not "grumbling and arguing," but "blameless and pure" (Philippians 2:14-15), letting our light shine.

> *We don't need to dominate conversations in order to get God's truth across.*

Making the most of every opportunity doesn't mean setting verbal traps to manipulate chats toward spiritual content. It means listening for the heart-needs of the people we're chatting with. "Let your conversation be always full of grace, seasoned with salt, so that you may know how to answer everyone" (Colossians 4:6).

As I've said throughout this chapter, listening is crucial. We need to hear what people are asking. We need to listen between the lines to sense what they're wondering, what they're needing. We need to be ready to respond with the love of Jesus.

Listening is crucial. We need to hear what people are asking, listen between the lines to sense what they're wondering, what they're needing, and be ready to respond with the love of Jesus.

"Always be prepared to give an answer to everyone who asks you to give the reason for the hope that you have. But do this with gentleness and respect, keeping a clear conscience" (1 Peter 3:15-16). Ironically, these words were written by Peter, who was known for rash actions and comments launched without thinking. But we all reserve the right to grow! This apostolic advice pulls together all three strands of our evangelism training. We live with hope, even in difficult circumstances. We listen and answer when people ask about our hope. And we speak the life-changing message of Jesus with gentleness and respect.

This passage clearly upholds the healthy tension of speaking and listening—while pointedly challenging the dominating that some evangelists practice in their sermons and some believers practice in their conversations. But on the other extreme, withdrawing is equally unhealthy. Too many believers have neglected the speaking part of this balance. They may listen well, but when the Spirit nudges them to speak a word of hope or love into someone's life, they hesitate, stay quiet, hedge their conversational bets, and can sometimes miss out on incredible God-moments.

They don't want to be rude, these Christians say. Why should they tell other folks how to live their lives? But people are asking in a lot of ways. They're wondering how you get through tough times, what propels you through life, and how you can embrace hope and love as you do.

It might be ruder to keep quiet.

CHAPTER 8

IN-TENSION-AL LIVING

One thing I love about the Bible is the way it connects with real life. It's not just a bunch of pious thoughts for some ethereal plane of existence. No, it's cutting-edge wisdom for the grit and grime of each day.

> *The Bible is not just a bunch of pious thoughts for some ethereal plane of existence. No, it's cutting-edge wisdom for the grit and grime of each day.*

As Moses gave God's commands to His people, he said, "Impress them on your children. Talk about them when you sit at home and when you walk along the road, when you lie down and when you get up" (Deuteronomy 6:7). He further invited them to incorporate God's Word in what they wore and how they decorated their doorways.

God pays attention to every aspect of our lives. "You know when I sit and when I rise; you perceive my thoughts from afar. You discern my going out and my lying down; you are familiar with all my ways" (Psalm 139:2-3).

The book of Proverbs applies God's wisdom to a wide range of detailed situations, and the prophets are stunningly specific in their critiques:

> *How terrible for you who sprawl on ivory beds and lounge on your couches.... You drink wine by the bowlful and perfume yourselves with fragrant lotions. You care nothing about the ruin of your nation.* —Amos 6:4-6 *(NLT)*

And, of course, Jesus told stories about fishers and farmers, sheep and goats, and runaways and homemakers. The Spirit leads real people through the ups and downs of everyday life, teaching us to keep our balance when the world threatens to topple us.

In that vein, after presenting six different healthy tensions, I want to explore them again, now applying them to six very important areas of modern life. It's not enough to understand the principle of, say, "speaking the truth in love." We need to do it, even when the forces around us make that difficult.

MARRIAGE (CANDID-KIND)

In a marriage, every one of our healthy tensions comes into play.

As two become one (see Mark 10:7-8), husband and wife need to find a common focus, and this requires a great amount of flexibility from both of them. They also need to find a rhythm of speaking and listening that both enjoy (withdrawing and dominating are early signs of a marriage in trouble). Couples also must balance their running and resting, finding activities they can share, and figuring out how much downtime they need—together and individually—to remain strong.

However, I want to zero in on the Candid-Kind tension. When it comes to speaking the truth in love, I can't think of any arena of life where that's more important than in marriage. Sadly, I've seen marriages turn bitter and critical, each partner taking every opportunity to expose the failings of the other. They might be speaking the truth, but love is long gone. They're candid but far from kind. Other couples never learn to talk about the hard truths of their relationship. Face it; "two becoming one" can be hard work. But some couples never face that fact. They breeze onward with flattering words that lose their meaning. They pretend everything's wonderful—until it's not.

Successful couples speak supportively while avoiding pretense. If there's a problem, they address it while not tearing down their partner.

I'm struck by two contrasting examples in Scripture. Delilah kept pleading with Samson to tell her the secret of his strength: "With such nagging she prodded him day after day until he was sick to death of it" (Judges 16:16). I've referred to that story at church, and there are always chuckles from couples in the congregation. They know that feeling very well. Of course, it turned out badly for

Samson—and it often turns out badly in modern marriages. When nagging—from either party—becomes the defining characteristic of a home, the balance between candid and kind begins to tip dangerously. (Quick tip for husbands: nagging may be a sign that she cares, but her silence is a sign that she's plotting your death.)

Consider, though, the picture in Proverbs 31. Yes, I know this offers an ideal image of a "superwoman" that seems impossible to achieve. I'll bypass the bits about making your kids' clothing, running a business, and speculating on real estate. I'm interested in what the husband says: "Many women do noble things, but you surpass them all" (Proverbs 31:29).

Over the years, I've heard many men complain about their wives, and many women complain about their husbands. To some extent, this is just blowing off steam in the company of trusted friends. But it's incredibly refreshing to hear a man say, "My wife is amazing! Let me tell you what she did for our family the other day!" The same is true when a woman shares how incredible her husband is, how grateful she is for him, and how attractive he is to her. (Who doesn't love a comment like that from their spouse?)

That kind of kindness, combined with honest communication within the home, makes for a strong marriage.

Kindness, combined with honest communication within the home, makes for a strong marriage.

IN-TENSION-AL LIVING

A marriage is the merging of two selves. Many people get married expecting to "complete" themselves. This idea has inspired all sorts of romantic lyrics and poetic notions—but it can be dangerous. Your spouse is not a shortcut to your self-actualization. He or she is also a self who may be seeking completion from you. The truth: no human being can complete another human being. Wholeness is found only in a true relationship with Jesus. The oneness of marriage is strongest when a man and woman who have found wholeness in Jesus are merging their two selves in a marriage with Jesus in the center. And until we find wholeness through Christ, every other relationship will be a misguided attempt to complete what only Jesus can complete.

Don't get me wrong. Both partners in a marriage should be self-aware, conscious of how they function within that union. Trouble arises when they're self-absorbed, focusing only on their own needs. Healthy marriages balance out the giving and the taking.

The pendulum swings back and forth in these relationships. Say, she faces pressure at work, so he picks up some of her home duties. Or he's sick in bed for a few days, so she does double duty with the kids. This is the normal ebb and flow of a committed relationship.

They maintain their balance by being both kind and candid. One spouse graciously gives time and attention to the other in times of need without hesitation. But at a certain point, that spouse may candidly say, "I've been giving and giving, and I need some support from you now." Grace is plentiful, but truth is also necessary. That's how marriages stay strong.

PARENTING (FOCUSED-FLEXIBLE)

You and your kids want the same thing, pretty much. You want to get them to a point where they can make wise decisions for their own lives, and they want that too. Except they want that *tomorrow*, and you know it will take a few more years... or decades.

If you're in the thick of it, I don't need to tell you about the challenges of parenting. It's a huge responsibility, and there are few parents who can confidently say they're doing it well. We make mistakes with our kids, and we just hope we don't scar them for life.

Once again, we could apply any of the healthy tensions of this book to the herculean task of parenting. The balance of speaking and listening is crucial. Many parents forget that as they try to transmit their own hard-won wisdom to the next generation. We forget that our kids need to win that wisdom for themselves. Yet open communication is vital for healthy homes. Smart parents learn to ask insightful questions and then stick around for the answers.

The balance of hope and realism also undergirds good parenting. Our hopes for our children are very high—stratospheric—but we also need to recognize who they really are—in their interests, their talents, and even their spiritual lives. We accept them always, and we nudge them forward.

In this chapter, though, I want to highlight the tension of focus and flexibility in parenting.

Some parents put all their effort into "laying down the law," and then they're at a loss when their kids break that law, ignore it, or dance around it. Without appropriate flexibility, a focus on discipline turns into dry rigidity. Don't misunderstand me here. Discipline is important, but never forget that it contains the word "disciple." Relationship is at the core of good discipline in the home. Kids are learning their responsibilities as members of a loving family.

Just as focus without flexibility leads to unhealthy rigidity, so flexibility without a focus on the responsibilities of family relationships leads to spinelessness. As I've observed over the years, kids really don't like the jellyfish life. When parents fail to set reasonable standards, it seems that they don't care.

I love what The Message does with the familiar "Train up a child" verse. "Point your kids in the right direction—when they're old they won't be lost" (Proverbs 22:6). I see focus here. Direction. Movement forward. Along with the realization that someday your kids will be walking that path on their own, making good decisions according to the instruction you have provided.

So how can you maintain flexibility in your home without going spineless?

Embrace the different roles you play as parents, especially at different times of the day.

Janet and I have learned to embrace the different roles we play as parents, especially at different times of the day.

Morning Time: We're their coaches. "Up and at 'em. Brush your teeth. Don't skimp on breakfast. You're not wearing that, are you? Do you have your homework? You're going to nail that test. There's the bus. Love you!"

Drive Time: We're their friends. On the way to or from soccer practice, youth group, or school, it's not the time for lectures. Just, "How are you feeling? Are you looking forward to this game? Did you have fun? What did you like best?" We can listen to the play-by-play of their lives with interest and empathy.

Mealtime: We're their teachers. No, we're not grading tests or assigning essays but processing the details of our lives. Our kids learn from us as we talk about our days, and we learn how they're applying the life principles we've taught them. (I know family mealtime may seem difficult to maintain with activities, conflicting schedules, and work or school responsibilities that just keep coming. But let me encourage you, find a few spaces in your week when your family can eat together some of the time. Maybe it's a weeknight dinner or two dinners and a Saturday brunch. There is tremendous value in meals shared together as a family.)

Bedtime: We're their counselors. We've always had a strict rule that our kids turn off all media at a certain time, but if they can't get to sleep, they can talk with us. Something about that time of the evening gets us all thinking about where we are and where we're going. We have treasured those late-night conversations.

You may find your flexibility in a different way, but do your best to be sensitive to the workings of their hearts and minds in different times and occasions. Don't sermonize when they need you to commiserate. Don't be a foe when they need an ally.

POLITICS (SPEAKING-LISTENING)

Politics has become such an omnipresent part of our culture that I can't avoid it. In general, many believe that religion and politics don't mix very well. When they do, it tends to "reli-tick" people off. Our faith certainly informs our citizenship, but political discord lacking healthy tension has not advanced the mission of the church as much as it's revealed our addiction to control—no matter the cost.

We should be troubled by the lack of civility in our civil discourse. It's worth repeating that we desperately need to heed the instruction of James: "Everyone should be quick to listen, slow to speak and slow to become angry" (James 1:19).

What I see is exactly the opposite. Quick to speak, with little listening. And zero to sixty on the anger scale in a nanosecond.

I know of a Christian teacher who writes a blog. In one post, she wrote something that upset some parents from her school. When one father wrote her an angry email, she suggested they talk about it. "No," he replied, "you'll just come up with some way to excuse what you wrote. I know you're wrong, and you can't convince me otherwise."

So much for "quick to listen." This wasn't, "Come, let us reason together" (see Isaiah 1:18); it was, "Don't even try."

That's the tone of a lot of conversations these days. Well, we can't really call them conversations, can we? We wind up comparing notes with those who agree with us and badmouthing those who don't. This is what we see and hear on TV, on social media, in our workplaces, and now, more than ever, in church.

I see three main tactics people use to avoid listening and to stir up anger in themselves and others. We've learned these "skills" from our news channels. Or maybe they've learned them from us.

Labeling

It's very easy to dismiss an opposing argument if you give it a negative label. A certain position is "socialist" or "fascist" or "elitist" or "anarchist" or "-phobic" in some way or "divisive." (I find that last one especially interesting. How can you dismiss someone else as divisive without being divisive yourself?) Labeling is shorthand. It's a shortcut around understanding. Once you've labeled somebody, you think you know what they're going to say, so why listen?

Attributing Motive

"They just want to...." How do you finish that sentence? The opposing group wants to seize power, take your power away, take your guns, replace you, create chaos, impose religion, destroy religion, steal elections, make life difficult for everyone who's not like them, or make it a crime to...."

You get the idea. In most cases, these ideas don't come from actual conversations with the people who supposedly want these things but from sound bites, assumptions, or willful misunderstanding. What do they really want? Why not ask them ... and listen?

Expanding

A TV anchor reported that a political candidate was vegetarian and then joked around with cohosts about it. If elected, would this candidate ban burgers? "I like my McDonald's," he declared, "and no one's gonna take that away from me!"

A simple, stupid, fun moment on TV, and yet it stirred up anger. It was designed to do so. It's absurd to think a candidate would or could ban burgers, but the simple news item was expanded into a threat. This sort of thing happens often in political discourse these days. We get mad easily—not because of what was actually said or done but because of what we imagine might happen next.

Christian love "does not dishonor others, it is not self-seeking, it is not easily angered, it keeps no record of wrongs" (1 Corinthians 13:5). Imagine what our political conversations would be like if we practiced that. You may lean right. You may lean left. But the Spirit of the living God invites you to "lean not on your own understanding" (Proverbs 3:5) and let the Lord's character and convictions guide your interactions.

> *You may lean right. You may lean left. But the Spirit of the living God invites you to "lean not on your own understanding" (Proverbs 3:5) and let the Lord's character and convictions guide your interactions.*

A healthy balance of speaking and listening is greatly needed these days. When we forget to listen, we dominate discussions—and we've heard plenty of that. Yet there are many others who have chosen not to speak, and instead, they withdraw from such discussions, even though they have sensible things to say. Let's all trust the Lord to guide us into loving discourse—quick to listen, slow to speak, and slow to become angry.

I appreciate the wisdom and tone of the Chris Rice song, "You Don't Have to Yell." In it, he suggests that everyone just take a breath and cool down. The yellers are red-faced, and listeners can't even distinguish the words that they're saying anyway. Rice makes the concession that, yes, things are worth fighting for, and people are naturally going to choose sides. However, "louder" doesn't make a person "right," so "You Don't Have to Yell."[2]

SOCIAL MEDIA (HOPEFUL-REALISTIC)

Everything I've said so far about marriage, parenting, and politics could also be said about social media. We desperately need to be candid and kind, posting the truth in love. We need to be *slow to become angry*. While we stay focused on our Christian identity, we can also deal flexibly with all the different things that come our way.

Seriously. Let this sink in. (We don't have to correct everyone's theology.)

> *Seriously. Let this sink in. (We don't have to correct everyone's theology.)*

But I want to zero in on one particular healthy tension—the balance between hope and realism.

The Internet, in general, is a wild place, and social media is its weird cousin. There's no accounting for what people will say or do—or record themselves doing. They do crazy stunts and goad others into copying them. They criticize every little thing you write.

---

2 Chris Rice, vocalist, "You Don't Have to Yell" by Chris Rice, July 17, 2007, track 5 on *What a Heart is Beating For*, eb+flo records.

They pick fights. They wax philosophical. They share strange theories. And on every birthday, you'll get well-wishes from people you didn't know you knew.

I mentioned in chapter 1 that Jesus once told His followers to be "as shrewd as serpents and as innocent as doves" (Matthew 10:16, CSB). That's a great principle for social media use. Let's be savvy about this. Don't get drawn into no-win arguments. Don't believe everything you read online. Maintain an active filter for deception and emotional manipulation. And, while some good relationships can be formed and developed on social media, be careful. By nature, these media tools make it seem like we know others deeply when we really don't have the full picture. In short, be realistic about the nature of social media, its limitations, and especially its dangers.

Increasingly, we find people addicted to social media. This is another danger to be wary of. If this is a potential problem, can you set limits on its use? Can you "fast" from it every so often and renew your involvement in the flesh-and-blood world?

Is there any hope for social media? Yes, absolutely! Wherever people gather, virtually or physically, there is opportunity for followers of Jesus to show and share His love. If loving one's neighbor as oneself is as important as Jesus says, then shouldn't we be looking for ways to do that? Suddenly, in this generation, we find our neighbors aren't just the people who live next door, not just colleagues at work, or not only friends at church. They also include every soul we interact with online.

So we have a new question to consider: How can we show the love of Jesus in that world?

I don't have a comprehensive answer to that, but I do have some ideas. Perhaps we should focus on value, fullness, and compassion.

In all our online interactions, we need to show and tell people that they have value. They've been created by God, they are loved by God, and that itself gives them tremendous worth.

There's a quote attributed to Fred Rogers, the minister who became the icon of children's TV, Mister Rogers. "Life is deep and simple, and what our society gives us is shallow and complicated."[3] This can apply to many parts of our society but none more so than social media. The conversation there can get very complicated, but it's usually quite shallow. By following the simple call of love, we can offer some fullness and depth to that world.

CHURCH (CONFIDENT-HUMBLE)

The one healthy tension I want to promote for church life is the balance between confidence and humility. Yes, we need focus and flexibility. Yes, we need candor and kindness and all the rest. But I feel our churches would thrive if we could be confident but not arrogant and humble but not ashamed.

A hallmark of the Christian life, humility gets great press throughout Scripture. "In humility value others above yourselves," writes Paul, going on to tout the example of Jesus, who gave up heavenly privilege for humanity (Philippians 2:3, 6-11). James adds, "Humble yourselves before the Lord, and he will lift you up" (James 4:10). Jesus commented on the Gentiles whose rulers lorded it over them. "Not so with you," He reminded His disciples. "Instead, whoever wants to become great among you must be your servant, and whoever wants to be first must be slave of all" (Mark 10:43-44). At the Last Supper, Jesus took a towel and washed the feet of His

---

3 Wendy Murray Zoba, "Won't You Be My Neighbor?" *Christianity Today*, 6 Mar. 2000, www.christianitytoday.com/ct/2000/march6/1.38.html.

IN-TENSION-AL LIVING

followers. "Now that I, your Lord and Teacher, have washed your feet, you also should wash one another's feet" (John 13:14). This is how things work in the topsy-turvy kingdom of God.

But we also have reasons for confidence—not in ourselves, but in the God who made us, redeemed us, and empowers us for His work. He has gifted us with certain talents, and it would be wrong to deny those.

Do you know where the word "talent" comes from? Originally it referred to a sum of money, the English rendering of a nearly identical Greek word. In the Parable of the Talents (Matthew 25:14-30), Jesus told about a master giving three servants different amounts of money—talents. But through the centuries, Bible readers understood that this parable wasn't just talking about money. The talents stood for all the gifts of God, including special abilities. Therefore, the English word talent took on that meaning. (So, next time you watch America's Got Talent, remember that the current meaning of that word comes from a Bible story.)

In that story, as you may know, two of the three servants invested their money-talents and doubled their holdings. The third, who buried his money-talent in the ground, afraid to lose it, earned the master's wrath. Our lesson is clear. We are urged to use whatever abilities or resources God has given us. It might seem humble to bury one in the ground, fearing that we might use it wrongly, but it's actually foolish. When God has equipped us, we can have confidence in God's equipping.

I have encountered a lot of wonderfully humble people at church. But I wish more of them would find confidence in the gifts of God and step forward to serve the church in adventurous ways. Confidence in God, rooted in humility about ourselves, is a powerful posture.

There's no room in the church for arrogance. When confidence in God turns to self-confidence, breaking its connection with humility, bad things happen. People stray, ministries fail, and the church staggers.

But we don't want to bury our abilities either. When shame steals our faith, keeping us from using the abilities God has carefully crafted for us, the church fades into passivity and irrelevance.

We need that healthy tension, taking the humble role of a servant yet confident in the bountiful gifts of God.

SPIRITUAL LIFE AND GROWTH (RUNNING-RESTING)

How do you feel about personality tests? Have you ever had a test that completely nailed it? "So *that's* why I do the things I do!" Or do you feel pigeonholed by these surveys? Or just confused?

I know many businesses have used the Myers-Briggs analysis, yielding sixteen personality types based on four factors. Others used the DISC profile based on another four factors. A number of Christian companies use the Strengths-Finder survey to identify dozens of possible personality types. I've heard both good and bad things about the Enneagram with its nine profiles. Now, you can even take a test to find out which Winnie the Pooh character you are... which Friends character you are the most like... and in case you're really desperate, which Desperate Housewife you are like. (I discovered I'm Tigger with a side of Chandler, possessing the poise of Deborah on Desperate Housewives of Milwaukee.)

In the last decade or so, I've seen more interest in how personality types affect a person's spiritual life and growth—not just their daily work. This is good.

For too long, preachers and teachers have insisted or implied that you need certain traits to grow spiritually. "Get up at 5 a.m. to read your Bible and pray!" If you're not a morning person, are you destined to lead a subpar spiritual life? "Get to know all your neighbors, and teach them about Jesus!" It's great when that happens, but introverts end up feeling very guilty.

People are wired differently. Some love to worship God outdoors. Others appreciate traditional forms of worship. Some have no problem giving their testimony in front of a crowd. Others prefer one-on-one interactions. Some visit sick people in hospitals. Others go on mission trips and build houses. You get the idea.

The six healthy tensions discussed in this book are just a few of the many different tendencies we find in the human family and in the Christian family. Every one of them affects the way you interact with God.

Let me hone in on one of the six: Running and Resting.

Christianity is an active faith. We are called to serve God and others, to offer our bodies as living sacrifices, using our God-given abilities in God's work (see Romans 12:1, 6-8). Isaiah promises that those who trust in God will "soar on wings like eagles; they will run and not grow weary, they will walk and not be faint" (Isaiah 40:31). James calls us to "be doers of the word, and not hearers only" (James 1:22, ESV).

I like that. I'm an active guy. I'm a doer.

If you're like me, you find yourself urging others to get with the program. "Wake up, people! Don't you see the task ahead of us? Let's get busy in God's work!"

But the Lord also says, "Be still, and know that I am God" (Psalm 46:10). God gave His people a weekly day of rest, the Sabbath. Even Jesus took time to go off by Himself to pray. "Come to me, all you who are weary and burdened," He said, "and I will give you rest" (Matthew 11:28).

> *So should we "be still" or "be doers"? If you've read this far in the book, you know the answer is "both."*

So should we "be still" or "be doers"? If you've read this far in the book, you know the answer is "both." Those of us who are always on the go need to slow down and smell the bacon. Those who prefer stillness or being alone should consider cranking up a little courage to interact with other believers and take their faith out for a spin.

There's a hard-to-translate passage in Habakkuk that gives us an appropriate pair of options. The prophet had some serious questions about what God was doing, letting the arrogant nation of Babylon rise to power and threaten Jerusalem. Habakkuk demanded an answer, and God complied: "Write down the vision and inscribe it clearly on tablets, so that one who reads it may run" (Habakkuk 2:2, NASB).

The idea seems to be that a messenger could read the message and then run to other villages with the news. But scholars can't quite agree on how the words read and run go together. Another version has "so that a runner may read it" (NRSV) with the idea that someone running past this writing could easily read it, and another translation says "so that it can be read at a glance" (GNT).

By the way, the message God was telling Habakkuk to write was an important one. Pride would cause the enemy's downfall, but the righteous would live by faith, trusting God and being faithful. This message (see Habakkuk 2:4) became a central piece of New Testament theology (quoted in Romans 1:17).

Still, I'm struck by the two translation options. Does the reader mull over this message and get energized by it, running to tell others? Or does the message catch the runner's eye as he rushes past, causing him to pause and meditate on the wise ways of God?

Perhaps both are necessary.

Runners, slow down and spend some serious time quiet in God's presence.

Readers, rise up from your meditations and take God's truth out to those who need it.

If you're a doer like me, you get impatient with interruptions. You don't like waiting. Yet God can meet you in that downtime—in the uncomfortable and seemingly inconvenient wait time—and beautifully nurture your spirit. I also know that those who rest in quiet reflection sometimes get annoyed when called to put their thoughts into action. It's like they're sitting quietly at a wedding reception when someone pulls them onto the dance floor. It might be uncomfortable, even scary, but this, too, is a way to grow your soul.

IN CONCLUSION

As we live our lives in our homes, schools, jobs, and churches, we experience the need for balance. As Christians, we talk about living in the world but not of the world, according to 1 John 2:15-16 (there's another healthy tension!), engaging authentically with people who don't follow Jesus but not growing attached to the current culture. We navigate by the wisdom of God's Spirit, stretching us this way and that, affirming who we are and pulling us toward growth, toward adventure. In our growing souls, we experience the healthy tension of a flexed muscle or a well-tuned guitar string.

"Keep in step with the spirit," Galatians 5:25 says. Some might think of that as a military march, but I think it's more of a dance. The Spirit pulls us onto the dance floor and leads us step-by-step.

CHAPTER 9

A PRAYER THAT'S TAUT

"I'm just not a church kind of person."

How often have you heard that? Even if your neighbors and coworkers aren't saying that in so many words, they might be thinking it. Some had bad experiences with church in the past. Some just never fit in. Some worry that they'll be judged for certain aspects of who they are. Many of these people aren't antichurch; they're just not "that kind" of person.

"What kind of person would that be?" you ask.

And that's where you get a truckload of different answers:

› "You know, those people who are all woo-woo about the Spirit."
› "They are just all about being strict."

> "They're confident they have all the answers, but I just have questions."
> "They're living in a fantasy land."

And so on. You can fill in more of what you've heard.

Maybe we deserve this. Maybe we've acted as if there's only one model for the perfect Christian, and if people don't measure up, we don't want them.

I hope you've learned the opposite from this book. God has created us with different temperaments, tendencies, and styles. The New Testament specifically mentions eyes and ears, hands and feet. Just as the body has different parts, the body of Christ has different people. Woo-woo or boo-hoo, sweet or sharp, confident or questioning—let's pool our personalities and bring it all before God.

> *Woo-woo or boo-hoo, sweet or sharp, confident or questioning—let's pool our personalities and bring it all before God.*

In that spirit, I've presented six different grids and quoted dozens of scriptures. There's not just one way to be, but in all these areas, it appears that a healthy tension between two different qualities is best. The Bible often warns against destructive extremes; there's a central range in which believers thrive.

I was delighted to see the same pattern emerging in the Lord's Prayer in Matthew 6:9-14 (KJV). In line after line, there's a pairing, explicit or implied. As I close this book, I'd like to parse this out.

Perhaps, as you repeat the Lord's Prayer in the future, you'll be reminded to keep these realities in a healthy tension.

Jesus made it clear that this was a prayer with meaning—not just a bunch of words to launch to the deity and not just a status symbol to show how religious you are. That's how pagans and hypocrites pray. No, we grapple with the substance of each line, offering not just our words but our very souls. Yet these words stretch our souls, stringing that tightrope across the chasms of our lives, balancing us, holding us together, keeping us whole.

WHO HE IS, WHO WE ARE

"Our Father, which art in heaven..."

When you discover who God really is, you get to discover who you really are. And in the very first two words of the Lord's Prayer, we get to see both. He is after personal, familial, relational connection. He's a father, I'm His child, and "we" are His children. The very first words of the prayer situate my connection to God vertically and to those around me horizontally because he's "our" Father.

He's also way above everything I can see. His perspective is a drone-shot view in contrast to my limited perspective on the surface of this tiny blue dot in the galaxy.

"Hallowed be thy name."

"He's God, and you're not." I heard of a pastor who spouted that phrase in nearly every counseling session. Whatever was ailing you, that was the cure. Temptation, doubt, marital difficulties—it always came down to the issue of who was ultimately in charge.

I'm not sure I'd apply that to every situation, but it's worth considering. We keep trying to take the controls of our lives, and we make a mess of things. The more we recognize that we don't belong on the throne, that we're not God, the better things will go for us.

As you probably know, hallowed is an old English word for "holy." But in the original Greek, it's a verb form, not a simple adjective. It means "to make holy." Literally, we're praying, "May your name be made holy."

But what does holy mean? If we say a human is holy, it means they're godly, like God, or in touch with God. A classic definition is "set apart for God." But what does it mean when we refer to God like that? God is godly? God is "set apart"?

I think we're telling God, "You are unlike anything else in my life. You are one of a kind. Nothing else compares to you. You are God—and I'm not."

Here's where we find our healthy tension. We can focus on how God is "set apart" from us, and many Christians do. I think of Isaiah's vision of God on His throne. The cherubim sang, "Holy, holy, holy," and Isaiah was ashamed of his own uncleanness (see Isaiah 6:1-8).

Scripture, though, also shows us a God who is intimately connected with us, not existing far away but drawing close. Even Isaiah found himself cleansed. God understands, forgives, and welcomes us into the family (see Psalm 103:12-14). Yes, He is "hallowed," but He's also "our Father." The holy God welcomes us into relationship.

And if He is "our Father," we are His children. We have great value—not because we have any holiness to boast of but because we've been created by a great God, redeemed by a Savior, guided by the Spirit, and welcomed into the family.

Can we become lax about His holiness, overly casual about our own sin? Yes, I've seen that happen. Others fear God in His holiness to the point that they're afraid to pray. Let's avoid both extremes. Let's hallow His holiness and also accept His invitation.

> *Let's hallow His holiness and also accept His invitation.*

HEAVEN AND EARTH

"Thy kingdom come. Thy will be done in earth, as it is in heaven."
We have two homes: heaven and earth.

I think of the old song, "This world is not my home; I'm just a-passin' through."[4] That echoes what Peter wrote about Christians being "temporary residents and foreigners" in this world (1 Peter 2:11, NLT).

In the same vein, the book of Hebrews hails heroes of faith:
> *They agreed that they were foreigners and nomads here on earth . . . looking forward to a country they can call their own . . . looking for a better place, a heavenly homeland. That is why God is not ashamed to be called their God, for he has prepared a city for them.* —Hebrews 11:13-16 (NLT)

Heaven is our true home, and this affects how we live on earth. Our priorities are not the same as those of other people. Our values

---
4 A. P. Carter, "I Can't Feel at Home Anymore," 1919, words in the public domain.

are different. We are "raised with Christ," and so we set our hearts on "things above" (Colossians 3:1).

Maybe you've heard the old line that some Christians are "so heavenly minded they're no earthly good." There's nothing wrong with longing for our heavenly home, but God also calls us to bloom where we're planted. We have the great examples of Joseph and Daniel, taken by force to new lands but investing their skills for the good of their new nations. Through Jeremiah, God gave a surprising message to the Jews in exile:

> *"Build houses and settle down; plant gardens and eat what they produce. . . . Also, seek the peace and prosperity of the city to which I have carried you into exile. Pray to the Lord for it, because if it prospers, you too will prosper."* —Jeremiah 29:5-7

And so we pray that God would carry out His plans, establishing His kingdom "on earth as it is in heaven." We live in healthy tension between our two homes. We know "our citizenship is in heaven" (Philippians 3:20), but we're also called to love our earthly neighbors and even those who make things difficult for us here on earth. God has not given up on this planet, and neither should we.

I like to take this verse one step further by remembering that we, as humans, are made from the dust of the earth. So when we pray, "Your will be done on earth as it is in heaven," we're asking God to work His will in us, in the dirt that He breathed into. "May your will, Lord, be lived out in me."

We have the opportunity to bring a heavenly perspective to our earthly dealings. We can speak peace into conflict, love into scorn, and truth into confusion. We value service rather than selfishness. We find joy not in shallow diversions but in the simple gifts of

God. We are ambassadors of heaven, reaching out to our fellow earthlings with a message of reconciliation.

GOD'S WILL AND OURS

"Thy will be done...."

Prayer is a battlefield for many of us. And I'm not talking about the prayer warriors whom I love and admire. I mean knowing what to pray for. Also, to be honest, there are too many preachers and authors telling people how to pray and how not to pray. I'm second-guessing myself whenever I go before God:

"Here's what I want, Lord, but 'Your will be done.' And I suppose You'll do what You want anyway, and that's fine with me, but this is the outcome I really want, if You don't mind."

I'm not making light of this; I'm just being honest.

I've had friends and relatives diagnosed with terminal cancer. I have prayed and prayed for a miracle cure. I'm sure you have experienced the same thing. We pray for healing, believing with all our hearts that God can step in and fix things. But in the vast majority of cases, we don't get the miracle we're praying for, or it looks very different than we expected, takes longer than we think it should, or has more complexities than we feel prepared to navigate.

Skeptics say, "Well, if God is going to do His will anyway, why pray?"

And I say, "Because He wants us to. Maybe it aligns our desires with His."

Some well-meaning teachers say, "Don't ask God for what you want. Just say, 'Thy will be done.'"

But the Lord explicitly invites us to "present your requests to God" (Philippians 4:6).

I've heard others say, "If you have enough faith, God will do what you want."

So it's up to me? I don't think so. Isn't faith all about trusting God to do what's best?

Like I said: prayer is a battlefield, with people lobbing half-baked theories like grenades. The casualties are immense. Too many Christians are intimidated by prayer, or they worry that they're doing it wrong.

I think God just wants to hear what's in our hearts.

> *I think God just wants to hear what's in our hearts.*

As a father, I know the joy of hearing my kids talk about their hopes and dreams—their "will." I've always loved this. And at various points, I've been able to help them get what they want... or to shape their desires... or to deal with disappointment. In all those cases, it starts with communication. It's built on relationship.

We can experience a healthy tension in prayer between our desires and God's. We saw this most clearly in the Garden of Gethsemane when Jesus Himself asked to be spared the suffering He was about to endure. He concluded, "Yet not as I will, but as you will" (Matthew 26:39).

Ask and accept. Plead, negotiate, and sweat great drops of blood. Let your requests be made known to God. Then trust that He will show His love and power in the most perfect way.

TODAY AND TOMORROW

"Give us this day our daily bread."

If you think of prayer as "asking God for stuff," note that we're halfway through this model prayer before we see a request. Not that there's anything wrong in asking—the Lord invites us to do this—but it's not like filling up an Amazon shopping cart and placing an order.

Our requests are rooted in relationship. Who God is and who we are. The way we both care about earth and heaven. What God wants and what we want. In that context, we ask God to meet our needs.

You probably remember the great miracle God worked to feed the Israelites as they journeyed through the desert (see Exodus 16). He rained bread from heaven. They'd wake up in the morning, leave their tents, and see the ground covered in these sweet confections, morsels of tasty bread. They didn't even know what to call it. They said, "What is it? What is it?" Eventually, they named it manna which is Hebrew for "What is it?"

God was answering the Lord's Prayer long before Jesus taught it.

Did you know that manna had an expiration date? It could not be kept overnight, or it would stink and get infested with maggots. (The one exception was the Sabbath day. God didn't want His people gathering food on the day of rest, so the pre-Sabbath manna would keep for an extra day. It was a miracle in a miracle.)

There's an important lesson in that fact, one that's repeated in the New Testament. We live a day at a time. We depend on God a day at a time. Of course, we love it when God provides assurances for the future. "Set me up with a bountiful IRA, Lord, and I'll be very grateful. I won't have to keep coming to you for 'daily bread.'"

But it seems that God likes providing for us each day. That's how we learn to trust Him.

> *It seems that God likes providing for us each day. That's how we learn to trust Him.*

Extremists might then question many of our common financial practices—savings accounts, insurance policies, retirement funds, etc. Shouldn't we trust God to provide?

That's something to think about, especially when we start worrying whether we'll have enough. Jesus said, "Do not worry about tomorrow, for tomorrow will worry about itself. Each day has enough trouble of its own" (Matthew 6:34).

And yet Scripture also calls us to live wisely: "The plans of the diligent lead to profit as surely as haste leads to poverty" (Proverbs 21:5). It only makes sense to plan for the future, but we also recognize that God has the final say: "Commit to the Lord whatever you do, and he will establish your plans" (Proverbs 16:3).

Jesus talked about planning: "Suppose one of you wants to build a tower. Won't you first sit down and estimate the cost to see if you have enough money to complete it?" (Luke 14:28). We should be quick to note that He was not giving business advice but urging His followers to consider the cost of discipleship. Still, He assumed it was a good and wise thing to plan for the future, even as He asserted His own call on people's lives.

The tension between today and tomorrow still occurs. We engage in a trusting relationship with God day by day. We rely on Him for spiritual, emotional, and physical sustenance. Yet we also make reasonable plans for the future—fully aware that God can change those plans in an instant: "Many are the plans in a person's heart, but it is the Lord's purpose that prevails" (Proverbs 19:21).

FORGIVEN AND FORGIVING

"Forgive us our trespasses as we forgive those who trespass against us."

In the Gospel accounts, Peter often seems like a ten-year-old kid, trying to figure things out and getting schooled by his Teacher. On one occasion (see Matthew 18), he rushed to Jesus and asked, "How many times do I have to forgive someone? Seven?"

Where did this come from? Was He chatting with a Pharisee or arguing with the other disciples? Maybe Andrew had already forgiven him twice for the same thing and refused to do so again. Apparently, Peter thought seven might be a better standard. It was a lot of forgiving, but Jesus was a very forgiving soul.

The Master's response must have blown his mind: "Not seven times, but seventy-seven times" (verse 22). Some older versions have "seventy times seven," but no one was counting up to 490. The point, clearly, is that we need to keep forgiving because God keeps forgiving us.

We need to keep forgiving because God keeps forgiving us.

As He often did, Jesus told a story to make His point. A servant owed the king a huge amount, but the king forgave that debt. Then the servant collared another servant and demanded repayment of a small debt. Hearing of this, the king severely punished the unforgiving servant.

The point is clear: Forgiven people need to forgive others.

This connection between receiving forgiveness and extending it pops up elsewhere in Scripture:

Bear with each other and forgive one another if any of you has a grievance against someone. Forgive as the Lord forgave you.
—Colossians 3:13

And Jesus emphasized it immediately after teaching the Lord's Prayer.

It's hard for a heart to open up to God's forgiveness when it is closed off to others. I've seen church people get caught up in scorekeeping, piling up their grievances against others. Sadly, this mindset often intrudes on their relationship with God. They keep trying to score religious points and avoid penalties.

But this is not the game God wants to play. He dismantles the scoreboard. Our righteous acts are like dirty laundry to Him (see Isaiah 64:6), but our sins are forgiven. And so are the sins of others. How can we hold grudges against people God has forgiven—especially when we are forgiven as well? God's kind of love, we learn, "keeps no record of wrongs" (1 Corinthians 13:5).

This pairing—forgiving and receiving forgiveness—is not a healthy tension as much as a fusion. Stop trying to split this atom. Forgive as the Lord forgave you.

LEADING AND TESTING

"And lead us not into temptation, but deliver us from evil. . . ."
Some Christians have trouble with this part of the Lord's Prayer. Why would God ever want to lead us into temptation? The Bible explicitly says that God does not tempt us (see James 1:13). So why would we have to ask Him not to?

It gets even more confusing when we note that the Greek word used in the New Testament for "tempt" can also mean test. In some cases, God allows testing to make us stronger (see Hebrews 11:17 and 1 Peter 4:12). The main difference between tempting and testing may be how we handle it.

"God is faithful," writes the apostle Paul. "He will not let you be tempted beyond what you can bear. But when you are tempted, he will also provide a way out so that you can endure it" (1 Corinthians 10:13). This is in keeping with what Jesus taught us. We can pray:

"Lord, I know you may allow difficult times in my life, but I don't want to be overwhelmed by them. If you lead me into these challenging situations, please lead me out as well. I want to keep following you through the whole ordeal."

A friend of mine is a public speaking teacher at a community college. Many of his students, he says, lack the money to go to a four-year college, and others went to substandard high schools or just didn't get the grades or the exam scores to get into bigger, better colleges. As a Christian, my friend sees it as his mission to help these students develop a valuable skill. Early in each semester, he tells the class, "It's my job to help you succeed. I'll test you, I'll critique you, and I'll challenge you. It won't be easy, but I'm not trying to trip you up. I'm fighting for your success."

He was surprised and deeply moved when a student came up after class and said, "I've never heard a teacher say that before. Thank you."

I think God is like that. He wants us to succeed, to grow stronger, and to pass the test. Yet He still allows us to face challenging situations. Some people get mad at God for this. Why can't everything be easy? Some blame God when they succumb to temptation.

But when we rely on Him to lead us out—to "deliver us from evil"—we grow.

The healthy tension here is between ease and difficulty. The Lord brings us great peace and joy, but we also go through hard times. We might want to deny or complain or blame God for our troubles, but we need to trust Him—even in "the valley of the shadow of death" (Psalm 23:4).

LISTEN UP

"Prayer is simply the key to everything we need to do and be in life."
—Tim Keller.[5]

Our identity, our priorities, and our perspective—they're all connected to our connection with God. "In him we live and move and have our being" (Acts 17:28). I mentioned at the beginning of this book that Jesus wants to help us find healthy tension and live in it. We're prone to extreme reactions, but Jesus is always inviting us back to a centered, surrendered trust in Him. Prayer is the way we stay connected—not just speaking to God but listening as well. This two-way communication with our Father in heaven

---

5   Timothy Keller, *Prayer: Experiencing Awe and Intimacy with God* (London, UK: Hodder, 2016) 18.

keeps us calibrated as we live here on earth in a way that honors the God of heaven.

In this model prayer, Jesus teaches us how to live.

> *Phrase by phrase, the Lord's Prayer tunes us. The healthy tensions of our lives are examined and counterbalanced with every line.*

Like a guitarist who makes necessary adjustments to the strings to produce the right sound, phrase by phrase, the Lord's Prayer tunes us. The tensions of our lives are counterbalanced with every line. Every time we pray it, we invite God to adjust the way we live, move, and have our being in Him.

In these final moments together, let's envision a man whose life was a magnum opus, his victories and defeats a living master class on tension. A shepherd and a sharpshooter. A poet and a political mastermind. A man after God's own heart, yet one who also struggled with extreme disobedience to God's will. The one and only: King David.

At the bottom of every towering mountaintop moment, there existed some deep dark valley along the spiritual topography of David's soul. Yet, God found him as He has found you. The Spirit of God led David in paths of righteousness just as He will lead you. Will you let Him?

Just as David would have pulled his ancient guitar close (a harp) and gently tuned each string, the King of all Kings wants to draw you close and bring you into harmony with Him. Just as David placed his fingers on the strings and produced a melody to complement the words, "Search me, God, and know my heart.... See if there is any offensive way in me" (Psalm 139:23-24), will you invite the King of your heart to do the same? If He has revealed areas that are out of tune or lack the proper tension, ask Him to recalibrate your heart. Only by doing this will we be able to remain balanced in the ongoing, ever-changing, consistently inconsistent pull between extremes and find full and vibrant life in Christ.

www.ingramcontent.com/pod-product-compliance
Lightning Source LLC
Chambersburg PA
CBHW070542090426
42735CB00013B/3050